ILLUSTRATED
DICTIONARY

T.AQUAIL MONTEZ
HARRIS

ILLUSTRATED DICTIONARY

Written by Betty Root

BACKPACKBOOKS
·
NEW YORK

Using this dictionary with your child

This colorful picture dictionary will be enjoyed by all young children. The very young will love to share it with an adult, talking about the lively pictures and giving names to the pictures they recognize.

Children who have just started to read will use the dictionary to understand the meanings of words and how to spell them. Some words may be unfamiliar; introducing those words will extend and enrich both spoken and written vocabulary.

The headwords (the words you look up) in this dictionary are in alphabetical order. Beside each headword you will see the part of speech—this tells you whether the word is a noun, an adjective, an adverb, or a verb. Each headword has a simple definition, an example sentence to help explain the meaning further, and an illustration. Care has been taken to ensure that the illustrations give the right clues to the example sentences.

Children will want to return to this dictionary again and again because it is both attractive and satisfying. The joy of using the dictionary will help children learn how to read many words and how to spell them. They will also learn that the world of words can be wonderful!

Betty Root

Aa Bb Cc Dd Ee

Ff Gg Hh Ii Jj

Kk

Mm

Oo

Qq

Contents

A–Z entries · · · · · · · · · · 10

The alphabet · · · · · · · · 213

Numbers · · · · · · · · · · · · · 214

Colors · · · · · · · · · · · · · · · 216

Shapes · · · · · · · · · · · · · · 217

Opposites · · · · · · · · · · · 218

Time · · · · · · · · · · · · · · · · · 220

Ll

Nn

Pp

Rr

Ss Tt Uu Vv

Ww Xx Yy Zz

Aa

abacus (noun)

You use an abacus to do math. It has beads that you slide along thin wires.

Can you use an abacus to add?

acorn (noun)

An acorn is a kind of nut. Acorns grow on oak trees.

Each acorn grows inside a tiny, brown cup.

accident (noun)

An accident is something bad that happens by mistake.

The boy had an accident on his bicycle.

acrobat (noun)

An acrobat is someone who can do exciting tricks. You watch acrobats at the circus.

The acrobat walked along the high wire.

add (verb)
When you add, you put two or more numbers together to make a bigger number.

If you add the numbers 3 and 7, the answer is 10.

address (noun)
Your address is the number of your house, and the name of the street and city in which you live.

You write an address on an envelope.

adult (noun)
An adult is a person or an animal who is grown up.

Parents and grandparents are adults.

afraid (adjective)
If you are afraid, you are frightened.

I am afraid of the big dog next door.

afternoon (noun)
The afternoon is the time between the morning and the evening. The afternoon ends at about 6 o'clock.

The children often play in the park in the afternoon.

air (noun)
Air is all around us. We all breathe air to stay alive.

You breathe air in and out of your nose and mouth.

a b c d e f g h i j k l m n o p q r s t u v w x y z

airplane (noun)
An airplane is a machine with wings. It flies in the sky.

People ride in airplanes to get to places quickly.

airport (noun)
An airport is the place where airplanes land and take off. They are always busy.

When you go away on vacation, you may go to an airport.

alarm (noun)
An alarm is a sound or a sign that warns you about something.

The fire alarm was ringing loudly.

album (noun)
An album is a book with plain pages. You stick photographs or stamps in an album.

My sister has an album of all her wedding photographs.

alien (noun)
In stories, an alien is a creature from another planet or from outer space.

Aliens often travel in flying saucers.

alligator (noun)
An alligator is a big, long animal. It has a thick skin and sharp teeth.

Alligators use their long tails to swim in lakes and rivers.

alphabet (noun)
The alphabet is the name for all the letters that we use to write words.

There are 26 letters in the alphabet. The first letter is a.

angel (noun)
An angel is a messenger from God. You read about angels in the Bible.

At Christmas, I was an angel in the school play.

ambulance (noun)
An ambulance is a vehicle that takes sick or injured people to the hospital.

An ambulance usually has flashing lights on the top.

angry (adjective)
Angry means very mad. People often shout when they are angry.

The giant was angry because Jack had taken his money.

anchor (noun)
An anchor is a heavy metal hook on a long chain. It digs into the bottom of the sea to stop a ship from moving.

The anchor hangs from the side of a boat.

animal (noun)
An animal is something that is alive and can move around. Plants are not animals.

Monkeys, parrots, snakes, and people are animals.

ankle (noun)

Your ankle is a part of your body. It is where your leg joins your foot.

Your ankle is a bone inside your leg.

antelope (noun)

An antelope is an animal like a deer. Antelopes live in Africa and in Asia.

You could not catch an antelope because it runs too fast.

annoy (noun)

If you annoy someone you make that person angry.

She annoys her teacher because she talks in class.

apart (adverb)

If two things are apart, they are away from each other.

Rachel was standing with her feet apart.

ant (noun)

An ant is a tiny insect. Thousands of ants live together in holes in the ground.

Ants often walk along the ground in a long line.

ape (noun)

An ape is a large monkey. It has long arms but no tail.

Apes like to eat leaves and fruits.

appear (verb)
When something appears it moves to a place where you can see it.

I like to watch when the full moon appears.

apple (noun)
An apple is a round and juicy fruit. Apples grow on trees.

Apples can be red or green. Which ones do you like to eat?

apricot (noun)
An apricot is a soft, round fruit. It has a big stone in the middle.

Do you like apricot jam?

aquarium (noun)
An aquarium is a large container made of glass or plastic. You keep fish inside an aquarium.

We have six fish in our aquarium.

archer (noun)
An archer is someone who shoots arrows from a bow. An archer usually shoots at a target.

The archer pulled back the string of his bow.

argue (verb)
When you argue with someone, you do not agree with what that person says.

My two sisters always argue with each other.

a b c d e f g h i j k l m n o p q r s t u v w x y z

arm (noun)
Your arm is the part of your body between your shoulder and your hand. You have two arms.

Do you stretch out your arms when you wake up?

armchair (noun)
An armchair is a very comfortable chair. It has sides so you can rest your arms on them.

Our cat likes to sleep in the armchair.

arrow (noun)
An arrow is a thin stick with a sharp point at one end. You use a bow to shoot an arrow.

I keep my arrows in a special case.

artist (noun)
An artist is someone who draws or paints pictures.

An artist usually stands up to paint.

ask (verb)
You ask a question when you want to find something out.

You put your hand up when you want to ask a question in class.

asleep (adjective)
When you are asleep you rest with your eyes shut. You do not know what is going on around you.

You are asleep at night in your bed.

astronaut (noun)

An astronaut is a man or woman who travels into outer space.

Some astronauts have walked on the Moon.

athlete (noun)

An athlete is someone who is good at sports such as running, jumping, or throwing.

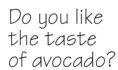

The athlete took part in a high jump competition.

atlas (noun)

An atlas is a book of maps. You find out where countries are when you look in an atlas.

I like to look in my dad's atlas.

avocado (noun)

An avocado is a fruit with a green skin. It has a very large stone inside.

Do you like the taste of avocado?

awake (adjective)

You are awake when you are not asleep. Your eyes are open and you know what is going on around you.

Are you wide awake each morning?

ax (noun)

An ax is a tool for chopping wood. It has a wooden handle and a sharp metal piece at one end.

You can chop down a tree with an ax.

a b c d e f g h i j k l m n o p q r s t u v w x y z

Bb

baby (noun)
A baby is a very young child. Babies do not walk or talk, but they can make lots of noise.

A baby often sits in a highchair to eat.

bad (adjective)
Bad means not good. It is the same as naughty.

Joe's sister was very bad when she burst his balloon.

back (noun)
Your back is the part of your body between your neck and your bottom.

You can see your back if you look in a mirror.

badge (noun)
A badge is something that you sew or stick onto your clothes. It shows which club or school you belong to.

I have a badge on my soccer shirt.

bag (noun)
You carry things in a bag. Bags can be made of paper, plastic, leather, or other material.

At the supermarket we put our shopping into plastic bags.

ball (noun)
A ball is round and bounces up and down. You play games such as soccer and baseball with a ball.

You have to kick a soccer ball hard.

bake (verb)
When you bake something you cook it in a hot oven.

My grandma bakes delicious cakes.

ballet (noun)
A ballet tells a story with dancing and music. It is a kind of play but has no words.

You watch a ballet on a stage.

balance (verb)
If you balance you keep yourself steady.

The acrobat had to balance on one leg.

balloon (noun)
A balloon is a small, thin bag. You can blow it up with air and make it bigger.

A balloon will blow away if you let go of it.

a b c d e f g h i j k l m n o p q r s t u v w x y z

banana (noun)

A banana is a long fruit with a thick, yellow skin. Bananas grow in bunches on trees.

You pull the skin off a banana to eat the inside part.

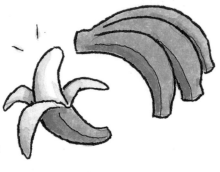

band (noun)

A band is a group of people who play music together.

The band played very loud music.

A band is also a thin strip of material. You use a band to hold things together.

She wore a band to keep her hair neat.

bandage (noun)

A bandage is a long strip of white material. You wrap a bandage around a part of your body that is hurt.

I've got a bandage because I cut my finger.

bank (noun)

A bank is a place where you can put your money to keep it safe. You can collect money from a bank too.

I put my birthday money into the bank.

A bank is also the side of a rive

The fisherman sat on the river bank to catch fish.

bar (noun)
A bar is a long piece of metal or wood.

A wooden bar keeps the barn doors shut.

bark (verb)
When a dog barks it makes a loud noise. Dogs bark when something worries them.

Our dog always barks at the mailman.

bare (adjective)
Bare means wearing no clothes.

You are bare when you take a shower.

barn (noun)
A barn is a big building on a farm. A farmer keeps animals or crops inside a barn.

In the winter, cows live in a barn to keep warm.

bark (noun)
Bark is the hard, outside part of a tree. It covers the tree's trunk and branches.

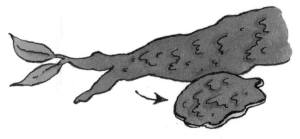

The bark of some trees has a pretty pattern.

baseball (noun)
Baseball is a game that you play with a bat and a ball. It is played on a field with bases.

In baseball you hit the ball with a long bat.

basket (noun)

You use a basket to hold things. Some baskets are made of thin, bendable wood.

My mom puts her shopping in a basket.

bat (noun)

A bat is a small animal with wings. It flies at night.

If you go into your yard when it is dark, you may see a bat.

A bat is also a wooden, plastic, or metal stick. You use it to hit a ball.

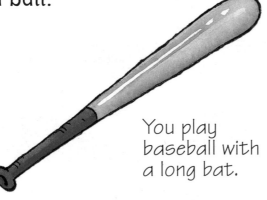

You play baseball with a long bat.

bathroom (noun)

A bathroom is a place where you can wash. It usually has a bathtub, a sink, and a toilet in it.

There is a big, white bathtub in our bathroom.

bathtub (noun)

A bathtub is a big container that you fill with water. You sit in a bathtub and wash yourself.

I like to play with my boat in the bathtub.

beach (noun)

A beach is the land next to the ocean. It is covered in sand or small stones.

You can build sandcastles on a sandy beach.

bead (noun)
A bead is a small, round piece of glass, wood, or plastic. It has a hole through the middle.

You can thread beads onto a string to make a necklace.

bear (noun)
A bear is a large, wild animal. Bears are furry and have sharp claws.

A bear is very big when it stands on its back legs.

beak (noun)
The hard part of a bird's mouth is called a beak. A bird uses its beak to find food.

A toucan has a very big, yellow beak.

beard (noun)
A beard is the hair that grows on a man's chin.

My dad's beard tickles my face when he kisses me.

bean (noun)
A bean is a long, thin part of a plant or a seed. You can eat some beans.

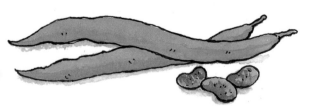

You usually cook these beans before you can eat them.

beautiful (adjective)
Beautiful means lovely to look at or listen to.

The sky looks very beautiful when the sun goes down.

a b c d e f g h i j k l m n o p q r s t u v w x y z

become (verb)
To become is to start to be something different.

A caterpillar becomes a butterfly.

begin (verb)
To begin is to start to do something.

I can begin to paint when I have my paint and brushes ready.

bed (noun)
A bed is something that you sleep in. Your bed is usually in your bedroom.

Does your teddy bear sleep in your bed at night?

believe (verb)
To believe is to feel certain that something is true.

Do you believe in the tooth fairy?

bee (noun)
A bee is a flying insect with six legs. Bees can sting you. Some bees make honey for you to eat.

Bees visit colorful flowers in your garden.

bell (noun)
A bell is a thick piece of metal like an upside-down cup. A bell rings when you hit it or shake it.

The bells in our school make a very loud noise.

belt (noun)

A belt is a long, thin piece of leather or plastic. You wear it around your waist.

You wear a belt to stop your pants from falling down.

bicycle (noun)

A bicycle is a machine that you ride on. It has two wheels that go around when you push the pedals.

I love my shiny, new bicycle.

bench (noun)

A bench is a long seat. It can be made of wood, metal, or stone.

The old lady likes to sit on a bench in the park.

big (adjective)

Big means something that is not small. An elephant is a big animal.

If your sweater is too big, it will cover your hands.

bend (verb)

To bend something is to make it curved. If you want to touch your toes, you have to bend your body.

Some magicians can bend spoons.

binoculars (noun)

You look through binoculars to make faraway things seem much closer. They are like two tubes joined together.

People use binoculars to watch birds high in the sky.

bird (noun)

A bird is an animal with feathers and two wings. Most birds can fly. Birds lay eggs.

Small birds will come into your yard if you hang out nuts for them.

birthday (noun)

Your birthday is a special day because it is the day you were born. You have a birthday every year.

What is the date of your birthday?

bison (noun)

A bison is a large, wild animal that lives in North America. It is a kind of buffalo.

A bison has a big, woolly head and thick horns.

bit (noun)

A bit is a small piece or a small amount of something.

The shipwrecked sailor stood on a tiny bit of land.

bite (verb)

To bite is to take hold of something with your teeth.

You bite an apple when you eat it.

blackberry (noun)

A blackberry is a dark, juicy fruit. You can find blackberries on bushes and in hedges.

We picked lots of blackberries to make a pie.

blackbird (noun)

A blackbird is a bird that you often see in gardens. Male blackbirds are black, but many female blackbirds are brown.

Most blackbirds have bright orange beaks.

blade (noun)

A blade is the sharp part of a knife or a sword.

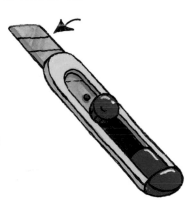

Be careful that you don't cut yourself on a sharp blade.

blanket (noun)

A blanket is a soft, warm cover. You often put a blanket on a bed.

I like to snuggle under my blanket.

blind (adjective)

A person who is blind cannot see.

Some blind people have a special dog to help them.

blizzard (noun)

A blizzard is a heavy snowstorm. Very strong winds blow in a blizzard.

If you go for a walk in a blizzard you could easily get lost.

blood (noun)

Blood is the red liquid inside your body. Your heart pumps blood around your body.

If you cut your finger, some blood might come out of it.

a b c d e f g h i j k l m n o p q r s t u v w x y z

blow (verb)
To blow is to push air out of your mouth.

You blow out the candles on your birthday cake.

boast (verb)
If you boast you talk too much about how you can do things better than others.

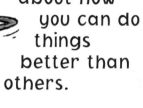

"I can do the best rope tricks," boasts the cowboy.

boat (noun)
You ride in a boat when you travel across water.

The Owl and the Pussycat had a pea-green boat.

body (noun)
Your body is every part of you, from your head to your toes. You usually wear clothes to cover your body.

A weightlifter has a very strong body.

boil (verb)
When a liquid boils it bubbles and gives off steam. If a liquid boils it is very hot.

You can see bubbles on the top of water when it boils.

bold (adjective)
Bold means brave. If you are bold you are not afraid.

The bold firefighter climbed the ladder.

bone (noun)

Bones are the hard parts inside your body. All the bones in your body make up your skeleton.

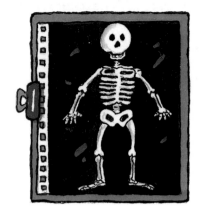

You have over 200 bones in your body.

boot (noun)

A boot is a strong shoe that covers your foot and your ankle.

You wear boots in the rain to keep your feet dry.

bonfire (noun)

A bonfire is a fire you make outdoors. It is dangerous to stand too near to a bonfire.

Dad burns dead leaves on a bonfire.

bored (adjective)

If you are bored you find something very dull and uninteresting.

I was bored because I could not play outside in the rain.

book (noun)

A book is made from pieces of paper that are joined together. A storybook has words and pictures in it.

Do you like to read a book at bedtime?

borrow (verb)

To borrow is to use something that belongs to someone else. After a while, you give back the thing you borrow.

If you forget your pen you can borrow one from your friend.

a b c d e f g h i j k l m n o p q r s t u v w x y z

bottle (noun)

A bottle holds liquids such as fruit juice and sauces. Most bottles are made of glass or plastic.

Bottles can be lots of shapes and colors.

bottom (noun)

The bottom of something is the lowest part of it.

When you go down a slide you stop at the bottom.

Your bottom is also the part of your body that you sit on.

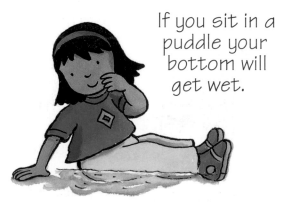

If you sit in a puddle your bottom will get wet.

bounce (verb)

When something bounces it jumps back after hitting something hard.

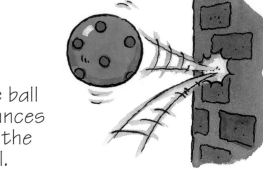

The ball bounces off the wall.

bow (noun)

A bow is a knot that has two loops.

Sarah wears pink bows in her hair.

A bow is also a long, curved piece of wood. You shoot arrows with it.

You pull the string of a bow to shoot an arrow.

box (noun)

A box is a container with straight sides. It can be made from cardboard, plastic, wood, or metal.

Do you keep your toys inside a box?

brain (noun)

Your brain is inside your head. You use your brain to think and have feelings.

Your brain helps you to remember things.

boy (noun)

A boy is a male child. When a boy grows up he becomes a man.

The boy is much smaller than his father.

branch (noun)

A branch is a part of a tree. It grows out from the trunk like an arm.

My rope ladder hangs from the branch of a tree.

bracelet (noun)

A bracelet is a chain or a band that you wear around your wrist.

Her bracelet was made of red and yellow beads.

brave (adjective)

Brave means not afraid. You are brave if you are not afraid of danger and pain.

The brave knight rescued the princess.

bread (noun)
Bread is a food made mainly from flour and water. You bake bread in an oven.

You can make toast with a slice of bread.

break (verb)
If you break something, it goes into smaller pieces.

"Did you break my tennis racket?" asked Joe.

breakfast (noun)
Breakfast is the first meal you eat each day. You eat it in the morning.

I always eat a bowl of cereal for my breakfast.

breathe (verb)
When you breathe you take air into your body and back out again. You breathe through your nose and your mouth.

You can blow hard as you breathe out air.

brick (noun)
A brick is a small block made of hard clay. You use bricks to build things.

We use bricks like these to build houses.

bride (noun)
A bride is a woman who is getting married.

The bride wore a long, pretty dress.

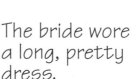

bridegroom (noun)
A bridegroom is a man who is getting married.

A bridegroom often wears a flower on his jacket.

bring (verb)
To bring is to fetch or carry something.

"Please bring your book to show me," said the teacher.

bridge (noun)
A bridge crosses over a river, a road, or a railway. A bridge lets you get to the other side.

Cars drive over a bridge but boats go under it.

broad (adjective)
Broad means very wide. It is a long way from one side of a broad street to the other.

It took a long time to row across the broad river.

bright (adjective)
Bright means easy to see. If something is bright it is not dull.

My favorite sweater is bright red and woolly.

brooch (noun)
A brooch is a small piece of jewellery. It has a pin at the back. You pin a brooch onto your clothes.

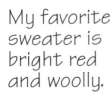

My brooch looks like a butterfly.

a b c d e f g h i j k l m n o p q r s t u v w x y z

a b c d e f g h i j k l m n o p q r s t u v w x y z

brook (noun)
A brook is a small stream.

The water in the brook is very clean.

broom (noun)
A broom has lots of hairs on the end of a long handle. You use a broom to sweep a floor .

You sweep leaves off the sidewalk with a broom.

brother (noun)
Your brother is a boy or a man. He has the same parents as you have.

My two brothers are bigger than me.

bubble (noun)
A bubble is a tiny balloon of gas. There are bubbles in soapy water and soft drinks.

Do you like blowing bubbles?

buckle (noun)
A buckle joins two ends of a strap. It is made of metal or plastic. You find buckles on shoes and belts.

This belt has a large silver buckle.

build (verb)
You build something by putting lots of different parts together.

My dad is building a new wall in the yard.

bulb (noun)

A bulb is the hard, round root of some plants. It is the part that grows under the ground.

A daffodil bulb has a yellow flower.

A bulb is also the glass part of a lamp. The bulb gives out light.

When you switch on a light the bulb starts to glow.

bulldozer (noun)

A bulldozer is a very big machine. It can move heavy stones and soil.

This bulldozer is working on a construction site.

bump (noun)

A bump is a round lump. If you knock your head you may get a bump on it.

Robert has a big bump on his forehead.

burger (noun)

A burger is a patty of ground meat. It is cooked and placed inside a bun.

Which kind of burger do you like to eat?

burglar (noun)

A burglar is someone who gets into a house and steals things.

The burglar climbed out of the window with his sack.

a b c d e f g h i j k l m n o p q r s t u v w x y z

bus (noun)

A bus is a large vehicle. It carries lots of people from place to place.

Do you go to school by bus?

bush (noun)

A bush is a large plant with lots of branches. A bush does not grow as tall as a tree.

Some roses grow on bushes.

busy (adjective)

A person who is busy has lots of things to do.

Daniel is very busy at work all day.

butterfly (noun)

A butterfly is a flying insect. It has four colored wings.

A butterfly sometimes spreads its wings in the sunshine.

button (noun)

A button is small and usually round. You have buttons to hold your clothes together.

You push a button into a hole or a loop on your shirt.

buy (verb)

When you buy something you give money for it. People often go to shops to buy things.

"I want to buy this bike," said Mom.

Cc

cabbage (noun)

A cabbage is a green vegetable. It is round and has lots of green leaves.

Caterpillars like to eat cabbages.

café (noun)

You go to a café to eat. You can buy food and drinks in a café.

You can sit outside this café on the sidewalk.

cactus (noun)

A cactus is a prickly plant. It grows in hot, dry places. Cactuses do not need much water to grow.

This cactus has brightly colored flowers.

cage (noun)

A cage is a big box with metal or wooden bars. People often keep birds and other small animals in cages.

Our pet hamster has a big wheel in its cage.

cake (noun)

A cake is made from flour, sugar, eggs, and butter. You mix these together and bake the cake in an oven.

A birthday cake has icing and candles on the top.

calculator (noun)

A calculator is a small counting machine. It can do math very quickly.

You use a calculator when you have to add a lot of numbers.

calf (noun)

A calf is a baby cow, a baby elephant, or a baby whale.

The calf is drinking milk from its mother.

call (verb)

To call is to shout out. You call out to someone so they can hear.

I call for my dog when I want him to come indoors.

To call is also to give a name to someone or something.

I call my pet rabbit Snowy.

calm (adjective)

If you are calm you are quiet. A calm person does not worry.

My mom is very calm when she lies out in the yard.

camel (noun)

A camel is a large animal with one or two humps on its back. Camels live in hot places.

You can ride on a camel but it isn't very comfortable!

camera (noun)

A camera is a machine that you use to take photographs.

Do you take a camera with you when you go on vacation?

canal (noun)

A canal is a kind of river. People make canals by digging them. A canal is usually straight.

Special narrow boats travel along on canals.

canary (noun)

A canary is a small, yellow bird. In some countries people keep canaries as pets.

Our pet canary likes to sing.

candle (noun)

When you burn a candle it gives you light. A candle is a round stick of wax. It has a string through the middle that you light.

Jacob had six candles on his birthday cake.

canoe (noun)

A canoe is a small boat that has a thin shape. You use a paddle to move it through water.

It is easy to fall out of a canoe, so you need to be careful.

cap (noun)
A cap is a small hat. People who wear a uniform often wear a cap.

I wear my favorite cap when I go out to play.

cape (noun)
A cape is a big coat with no sleeves. You put your arms through holes in the sides of a cape.

Witches and wizards wear big, long capes.

car (noun)
A car is a vehicle with an engine and wheels. You drive a car along a road.

My dad has a new, red car.

card (noun)
A card is something that you send to someone on their birthday. It has a picture on the front and words inside.

I had lots of cards on my 7th birthday.

cardboard (noun)
Cardboard is thick paper. It does not bend easily. Cardboard is used to make boxes.

Cereal boxes are made from cardboard.

carpet (noun)
A carpet is a thick, soft cover for the floor. When you walk on a carpet you do not make a noise.

We have a green carpet in our hall.

carrot (noun)
A carrot is a long, thin vegetable. It grows under the ground. You can eat it uncooked or cooked.

Rabbits like to eat carrots.

carry (verb)
To carry is to take something to another place. When you carry something you pick it up first.

Our teacher always carries a big pile of books.

cartoon (noun)
A cartoon is a kind of film. It has moving drawings instead of real people.

We watch cartoons on the television.

case (noun)
A case is a container that you keep things in. You can also use a case to carry things around.

I keep my colored pencils in a pencil case.

cassette (noun)
A cassette is a small plastic box with a tape inside it. The tape has music or stories on it.

You need to play a cassette inside a cassette player.

castle (noun)
A castle is a big building with thick, stone walls. People built castles to keep out dangerous enemies.

This old castle is falling down.

a b c d e f g h i j k l m n o p q r s t u v w x y z

cat (noun)

A cat is a small, furry animal. It has a long tail. Some people keep cats as pets.

My cat likes to play with a ball of wool.

catch (verb)

To catch is to take hold of something when it is moving. You catch with your hands.

If someone throws a ball you try to catch it.

caterpillar (noun)

A caterpillar is like a furry worm. Caterpillars change into butterflies and fly away.

Look for a caterpillar on a leaf in your garden.

cave (noun)

A cave is a large hole in the side of a hill or cliff. There are also caves under the ground.

You would need a flashlight inside a cave because it is dark.

CD (noun)

CD is short for compact disc. It is a thin, silver circle. You can hear music when you put a CD inside a CD player.

You can fit a compact disc on your hand.

ceiling (noun)

A ceiling is the highest part of a room. You cannot reach the ceiling unless you are very tall.

My bedroom ceiling has lots of stars on it.

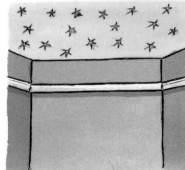

center (noun)
The center is the middle of something.

The flowers are in the center of the table.

chain (noun)
A chain is made from metal or plastic rings that are joined together. Some chains are very heavy and strong.

The chain was made of gray metal.

chair (noun)
A chair is something that you sit on. Some chairs have four legs and a back.

Goldilocks is sitting in Daddy Bear's big chair.

chalk (noun)
A chalk is a stick of soft rock. Most chalks are white. You use chalk to write on a chalkboard.

In the box there are many different colors of chalk.

change (noun)
When you pay too much for something the money you get back is called change.

The ice cream man gave me some change.

change (verb)
To change is to make something different. You change your book at the library to get a different one.

My little sister likes to change her clothes a lot.

chase (verb)
To chase is to run after someone or something.

Our dog likes to chase cats.

chat (verb)
To chat is to talk to someone in a friendly way. When you chat you do not talk about important things.

Grandma likes to chat when she goes to the drug store.

cheap (adjective)
If something is cheap it does not cost a lot of money.

The bananas in the market are very cheap.

cheer (verb)
To cheer is to shout out loud when you are excited or happy.

Do you like to cheer for your favorite team?

cheese (noun)
Cheese is a food made from milk. It can be hard or soft. Some cheeses smell very strong.

This kind of cheese has holes in it.

cherry (noun)
A cherry is a small, round fruit. A cherry has a hard stone in the middle. You must not eat the stone!

A cherry can be red or black.

chess (noun)
Chess is a board game for two people. Each player has 16 pieces. You have to think hard when you play chess.

In chess, you play with a black and white board.

chick (noun)
A chick is a baby bird. It can be any kind of bird.

There are four hungry chicks in this nest.

chest (noun)
Your chest is the front part of your body between your neck and your stomach.

Your chest moves in and out when you breathe.

chicken (noun)
A chicken is a farm bird that does not fly. Mommy chickens lay eggs.

A mommy chicken is called a hen, and a daddy chicken is called a rooster.

A chest is also a very strong box. You keep things in it. Chests are usually made of wood or metal.

Pirates used to keep their treasure in a chest.

child (noun)
A child is a young boy or girl. Children have not grown up.

The teacher held hands with each child.

chimpanzee (noun)

A chimpanzee is an animal with long arms and no tail. It is a kind of ape. Chimpanzees live in Africa.

The chimpanzee likes to swing in the tree.

chin (noun)

Your chin is the part of your face under your mouth. You have a bone in your chin.

If you touch your chin it feels very hard.

chocolate (noun)

Chocolate is a sweet food. It is made from cocoa and sugar.

Chocolate goes soft and sticky if you hold it in your hands.

choir (noun)

A choir is a group of people who sing together.

My sister sings in a choir at school.

choose (verb)

To choose is to pick something you want to have or do.

I take a long time when I choose which clothes to wear.

chop (verb)

To chop is to cut something into pieces. You use a knife or an ax to chop things.

The lumberjack chopped down the old tree.

church (noun)
A church is a building where some people go to pray. Some churches are very big.

Our church has lots of colored windows.

clap (verb)
To clap is to hit your hands together to make a noise.

My baby sister likes to clap.

circus (noun)
A circus is a show with clowns and acrobats. A circus moves from one place to another.

You watch a circus inside a big tent.

class (noun)
A class is a group of children who learn together.

There are 20 children in my class at school.

city (noun)
A city is a very big town. There are usually many tall buildings in a city.

There are lots of cars and trucks in this city.

clean (adjective)
When something is clean it is not dirty.

You can make your face clean with a cloth and warm water.

clear (adjective)
If something is clear it is easy to see through it.

You can see through glass because it is clear.

cling (verb)
If you cling to something, you hold onto it tightly.

The windsurfer clings to a bar as he moves along.

cliff (noun)
A cliff is a high hill that can be near the ocean. Most cliffs are made of rock.

The cliff behind the beach was very steep.

clock (noun)
A clock is a machine that tells what time it is. The clock's hands point to the right time.

An alarm clock makes a loud noise to wake you.

climb (verb)
When you climb you use your hands and feet to go up something.

Could you climb these monkey bars?

close (verb)
To close something is to shut it.

"Please close the door behind you!" said the teacher.

clothes (noun)
All the things you wear on your body are clothes.

Skirts, pants, and T-shirts are clothes.

coal (noun)
Coal is a hard, black rock. You dig coal out of the ground and burn it in a fire.

A sack of coal is very dusty.

cloud (noun)
A cloud is a patch of white, gray, or black in the sky. It is made of many little drops of water.

Rain comes down from clouds.

coat (noun)
You wear a coat on top of your clothes when you go outside.

A coat keeps you warm when it is cold.

clown (noun)
A clown is a person who dresses up and does funny tricks.

Clowns do silly things to make people laugh.

cobweb (noun)
A cobweb is a sticky net. It is made by a spider to catch flies to eat.

This spider has three flies in its cobweb.

coconut (noun)

A coconut is a very big, brown nut. It grows on tall trees in hot countries. Inside the hard shell are white flesh and milk.

It is difficult to break open a coconut.

coin (noun)

A coin is a small piece of money. Coins are made from metal.

This coin has a picture of a bird on it.

cold (adjective)

When something is cold it is not hot. It is cold when there is snow.

Do you get cold when you build a snowman?

cold (noun)

If you have a cold you are sick. You have to blow your nose a lot.

When I have a cold I always sneeze a lot.

collar (noun)

A collar is the part of a shirt or a coat that goes around your neck.

Dad turns up his collar when it is windy.

color (noun)

A color is the way that something looks in daylight. Red, blue, and green are colors.

My paintbox has eight different colors in it.

comb (noun)
You use a comb to keep your hair neat. It is a flat piece of plastic or metal with thin teeth.

My sister has a pretty, pink comb.

compass (noun)
A compass helps you find out where you are going. It has a needle that always points to the north.

An explorer uses a compass.

come (verb)
To come is to move toward something or someone.

"Come over here!" called Mom.

computer (noun)
A computer is a machine that stores lots of information. People use computers in stores, offices, and schools.

You use a keyboard with a computer.

comic book (noun)
A comic book tells stories and jokes in pictures. It is like a small newspaper or magazine.

Which is your favorite comic book?

connect (verb)
To connect is to join two things together.

I can connect a printer to my computer.

a b c d e f g h i j k l m n o p q r s t u v w x y z

cook (verb)

When you cook you make food ready to eat. You cook by heating the food.

I like it when I can cook at school.

copy (verb)

To copy is to do the same as someone else.

Twins like to copy each other.

corner (noun)

A corner is the place where two edges meet. Two streets meet at a corner.

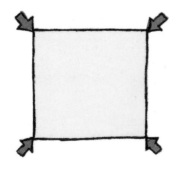

A square has four corners.

cottage (noun)

A cottage is a small house. You find cottages in the country, not in the towns.

This cottage is made of brick.

count (verb)

To count is to find how many things there are.

I like to count the ducks on the pond.

To count is also to say numbers in order.

1 2 3 4 5 6 7 8 9 10

My little brother can count up to ten.

cow (noun)

A cow is a large, farm animal. Milk comes from mommy cows.

A daddy cow is called a bull.

cowboy (noun)

A cowboy is a man who looks after cattle. A cowboy usually works on a ranch.

A cowboy usually rides on a horse.

crab (noun)

A crab is an animal with a hard shell. It has two claws and eight legs.

Have you ever seen a crab on the beach?

crack (noun)

A crack is a thin line on something that is nearly broken.

My mug has a big crack in it.

cracker (noun)

A cracker is a thin, crisp biscuit. You can eat crackers with soup or cheese.

Lots of crackers are square, like these ones.

crane (noun)

A crane is a big machine with a long arm. It can lift very heavy things.

The crane is lifting a very heavy pipe.

crash (noun)
A crash is a loud noise. It happens when something falls or breaks.

The vase fell on the floor with a loud crash.

crash (verb)
Two cars crash if they bump into each other.

I crashed into the wall on my bicycle.

crawl (verb)
To crawl is to move along on the ground by using your hands and knees.

Babies crawl before they can walk.

crayon (noun)
You use a crayon to draw a picture. It is a stick made of colored wax.

I drew a cat with my green crayon.

crisp (adjective)
Crisp means hard and firm. Something that is crisp breaks easily.

I like to eat crackers that are crisp.

crocodile (noun)
A crocodile is a long animal. It has lots of sharp teeth and a very strong tail.

Crocodiles swim in rivers in hot countries.

crooked (adjective)
Crooked means bent or twisted.

The old man had a crooked cane.

cross (adjective)
When you are cross you feel angry. Your face tells people that you are cross.

My sister was cross when I broke her mirror.

crowd (noun)
A crowd is a lot of people in the same place. You can get lost in a busy crowd.

There was a big crowd outside the movie theater.

crown (noun)
A crown is a ring of gold or silver. Kings and queens wear a crown on their head.

The gold crown had rubies and diamonds on it.

cry (verb)
You cry when you are hurt or you feel sad.

Tears run down your face when you cry.

cucumber (noun)
A cucumber is a long, thin fruit. It has a green skin and is soft and white inside.

You can cut a cucumber into very thin slices.

cuddle (verb)

When you cuddle someone you put your arms around that person. You cuddle in a friendly way.

I cuddle my teddy bear at night.

cup (noun)

A cup is a small bowl with a handle. You put drinks such as tea or coffee into a cup.

A cup usually stands on a saucer.

cupboard (noun)

A cupboard is a place in a kitchen where you keep things. It has a door on the front and shelves inside.

Do you keep your pans in a cupboard like this?

curtain (noun)

A curtain is a piece of material that hangs by a window. You pull a curtain across the window to cover it.

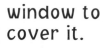

My bedroom curtains have rockets and stars on them.

cushion (noun)

A cushion is a soft pillow. You put cushions on a sofa or on a chair. It is more comfortable when you sit on a cushion.

The armchair has two big, red cushions.

cut (verb)

When you cut something you open or divide it. You can use a knife or scissors to cut.

I'll cut the pizza into six slices.

Dd

daisy (noun)

A daisy is a small flower. It has white or pink petals and a yellow middle. Daisies often grow in grass.

You can join daisies together to make a daisy chain.

damp (adjective)

If something is damp it feels a little wet.

My sweater is damp because I left it out in the yard.

dam (noun)

A dam is a wall that is built across a river. It holds back water.

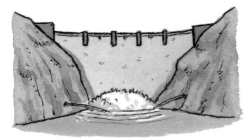

The dam was made of thick stones.

dance (verb)

To dance is to move about in time to music.

I love to dance with my friend.

a b c d e f g h i j k l m n o p q r s t u v w x y z

danger (noun)
Danger means something that is not safe. If there is danger you may get hurt.

The fishing boat was in danger among the huge waves.

dark (adjective)
Dark means that it is not light.

You use a flashlight at night because it is dark outside.

dawn (noun)
Dawn is early in the morning. It starts to get light at dawn.

Birds start to sing when it is dawn.

day (noun)
A day is 24 hours. It lasts from midnight to the midnight of the next day.

There are 7 days in one week.

deaf (adjective)
A person who is deaf cannot hear very well. Some deaf people cannot hear at all.

You need to speak clearly to a deaf person.

decorate (verb)
If you decorate something, you add things to make it look pretty.

We like to decorate our front door with balloons and streamers.

a b c d e f g h i j k l m n o p q r s t u v w x y z

deep (adjective)
If something is deep it goes down a long way from the top.

I can dive into the swimming pool at the deep end.

deer (noun)
A deer is a wild animal that can run very fast. Deer often live in the woods.

A male deer has big horns.

deliver (verb)
If you deliver something you take it to someone's home or office.

The mailman delivered a big package on my birthday.

dentist (noun)
A dentist is a person who takes care of your teeth. A dentist can stop your tooth from hurting.

When you go to the dentist you sit in a big chair.

desert (noun)
A desert is a very dry place. Only a few plants and animals live in deserts. Most deserts are hot places.

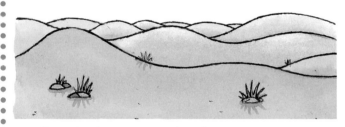

The Sahara is the biggest desert in the world.

desk (noun)
A desk is a table with drawers. A computer sometimes sits on a desk.

You sit at a desk to work.

a b c **d** e f g h i j k l m n o p q r s t u v w x y z

dessert (noun)

A dessert is a sweet food that you eat at the end of a meal.

Ice cream is my favorite dessert.

diamond (noun)

A diamond is a hard, clear stone that sparkles. Diamonds are jewels and they cost a lot of money.

The gold ring had a large diamond in it.

dice (noun)

Dice have six sides with different numbers of dots on each side.

You throw dice when you play a board game.

dictionary (noun)

A dictionary is a book that tells you what words mean. You also use a dictionary to find out how to spell words.

Which words did you look up in this dictionary?

dig (verb)

To dig is to make a hole in soil or sand. You can use a shovel to dig.

A dog uses its paws to dig in the yard.

dinosaur (noun)

A dinosaur is a very large animal that lived a very long time ago. There are no dinosaurs alive today.

We know that some dinosaurs were as tall as big trees.

dirty (adjective)
When something is dirty it is not clean.

If your sneakers are covered in mud they are dirty.

dislike (verb)
If you dislike, you do not like someone or something.

He really dislikes eating fish.

disco (noun)
A disco is a place where you go to dance to music.

We like to dance at the disco.

dive (verb)
To dive is to jump into water head first.

Penguins can dive into very cold water.

dish (noun)
A dish is a container that you put food in. Dishes are made out of china or glass.

There is a large dish of vegetables on the table.

diver (noun)
A diver is a person who goes under water. A diver wears a special rubber suit to keep warm.

The diver found a big crab at the bottom of the ocean.

a b c **d** e f g h i j k l m n o p q r s t u v w x y z

divide (verb)
To divide means to separate into smaller parts.

Mom divided the flowers into two bunches.

doctor (noun)
A doctor is a person who takes care of you when you are sick. Doctors try to make people feel better.

A doctor will visit you if you are in the hospital.

dog (noun)
A dog is a furry animal with four legs. Many people have dogs as pets.

Dogs come in lots of different sizes and colors.

doll (noun)
A doll is a toy that looks like a baby, a child, or an adult.

My favorite doll has long, blond hair.

dolphin (noun)
A dolphin is an animal that lives in the ocean. Dolphins are very smart and are often friendly.

If you're lucky you can watch dolphins jumping out of the water.

domino (noun)
A domino is a plastic or wood block with dots on it. You play a game with dominoes. Some dominoes have pictures instead of dots.

You match the dots when you play with dominoes.

donkey (noun)

A donkey is an animal that looks like a small horse. Donkeys have long ears.

Have you ever had a ride on a donkey?

dove (noun)

A dove is a bird. It looks a bit like a pigeon.

A dove makes a quiet noise that goes "coo, coo."

door (noun)

A door lets you go in and out of a room, a house, or a car. You open or close a door to go through it.

Our front door is bright green.

dragon (noun)

A dragon is not a real animal. You can read about dragons in storybooks.

In stories, dragons usually breathe fire.

dot (noun)

A dot is a small, round mark.

She started to connect the dots on the board.

draw (verb)

When you draw, you make a picture or a pattern with a pencil or crayon.

My brother can draw really well.

drill (noun)
A drill is a tool for making holes.

It is quicker to make holes when you use an electric drill.

drum (noun)
A drum is a musical instrument. You hit a drum with two sticks to make a sound.

I can make lots of noise when I play my drum.

drink (verb)
When you drink you put liquid into your mouth and swallow it.

I like to drink strawberry milk shakes.

dry (adjective)
Dry means not wet.

You stay dry in the rain if you use an umbrella.

drive (verb)
To drive is to make a car go where you want it to go.

People also drive buses, trains, and trucks.

My uncle drives a big, blue truck.

duck (noun)
A duck is a bird that can swim and fly. It has special feet to help it swim.

I like to feed the ducks in the park.

E e

eagle (noun)

An eagle is a very large bird. Eagles hunt and eat mice and rabbits.

You will not see an eagle in your backyard!

early (adjective)

If you are early you arrive in plenty of time for something. Early means not late.

If I get to school early I have to wait outside the gate.

ear (noun)

An ear is a part of your head. You have two ears and they help you hear.

You use your ears to hear all the sounds around you.

eat (verb)

When you eat you put food in your mouth. To eat your food, you chew and then swallow it.

What do you like to eat for dinner?

a b c d **e** f g h i j k l m n o p q r s t u v w x y z

egg (noun)
A bird's egg has a hard shell. A baby bird starts to grow inside it. Birds, fish, and insects lay eggs.

A baby chick has to break out of its egg.

elephant (noun)
An elephant is a very large animal. It has big, floppy ears and lives in the jungle.

An elephant is the biggest animal that lives on land.

elbow (noun)
An elbow is a hard, bony part of your arm. It is where your arm bends.

You have to bend your elbows when you lift something heavy.

empty (adjective)
Something that is empty has nothing inside it.

Your glass is empty when there is no more orange juice in it.

electricity (noun)
Electricity gives us light and heat. It is a kind of energy. Electricity makes lots of machines work.

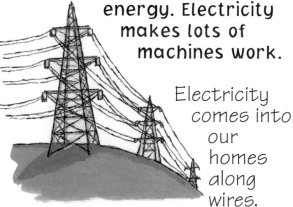

Electricity comes into our homes along wires.

enter (verb)
To enter is to go into a place. You enter a room through a door.

I see lots of toys when I enter the toy store.

envelope (noun)
An envelope is a paper covering for a letter. You put a letter inside it.

You write an address on an envelope and stick a stamp on it.

escape (verb)
To escape is to get away from something or somebody. If you escape you are free.

The hamster escaped from its cage.

equal (adjective)
Equal means the same number or the same size.

You have an equal number of fingers on each hand.

evening (noun)
The evening is the early part of the night. It comes at the end of the afternoon.

The sun goes down in the evening and it becomes dark.

escalator (noun)
An escalator is a moving staircase. You see escalators in big stores and in airports.

It is easier to go on the escalator than to walk down the stairs.

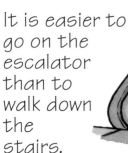

eye (noun)
You have two eyes on your face. You see with your eyes.

What color are your eyes?

a b c d e f g h i j k l m n o p q r s t u v w x y z

Ff

face (noun)
Your face is the front part of your head. Your nose, eyes, and mouth are on your face.

You can see your face when you look in a mirror.

fairy (noun)
A fairy is not a real person but someone you read about in stories. Fairies have wings and are often very small.

A fairy waves her wand to do magic things.

factory (noun)
A factory is a big building where things are made. Lots of people usually work inside a factory.

Cars are made inside this factory.

fall (verb)
To fall is to drop down quickly. If you fall you might hurt yourself.

Sometimes the apples fall off the tree onto the ground.

abcdefghijklmnopqrstuvwxyz

family (noun)
A family is a group of people. It is made up of one or two parents and children.

There are five people in my family. How many are in yours?

fan (noun)
A fan is a machine that blows air when it moves. Fans blow hot or cold air.

She had a fan on her desk to keep cool.

far (adjective)
Far means a long way away. If something is far it takes a long time to get there.

The Moon is far away from the Earth.

farm (noun)
A farm is a large piece of land with buildings on it. On a farm people keep animals and grow crops for food.

Cows, pigs, and chickens live on this farm.

farmer (noun)
A farmer looks after a farm. A farmer drives a tractor, feeds the animals, and looks after the fields.

The farmer is feeding a baby lamb.

fast (adjective)
Fast means quick. Something that is fast is not slow.

Jim is a very fast runner and wins lots of races.

a b c d e f g h i j k l m n o p q r s t u v w x y z

fat (adjective)
Fat means big all over. A fat animal is not thin.

Some monsters are fat because they eat a lot of food.

father (noun)
A father is a man who has children. He is a male parent.

Most children call their father "Dad."

fear (verb)
To fear something is to be afraid of it.

The knight began to fear the fierce dragon.

feather (noun)
A bird has lots of feathers all over its body. Feathers keep birds warm. They also help most birds fly.

Some feathers have lots of very bright colors.

feel (verb)
To feel something is to touch it gently.

I like to feel the soft fur on my rabbit.

female (adjective)
A female person or animal can have babies or lay eggs.

A female lion is called a lioness.

a b c d e (f) g h i j k l m n o p q r s t u v w x y z

70

fence (noun)
A fence is a kind of wall made from wood or wire. A fence runs around a field or a yard.

A rose plant grows up our fence.

find (verb)
To find is to come across someone or something that you are looking for. You are pleased when you find something.

Mom was happy to find the keys in her purse.

fetch (verb)
To fetch is to go and get something. When you fetch something you take it to someone else.

The dog ran off to fetch the ball.

finger (noun)
A finger is part of your hand. You have four fingers and a thumb on each hand.

You can use your fingers to help you count.

field (noun)
A field is a piece of land with a hedge, a wall, or a fence around it. Grass or crops grow in a field.

The horse eats the grass in the field.

fire (noun)
A fire is the flames that are made when something burns. A fire can keep you warm.

A fire can be dangerous if you go too near it.

a b c d e f g h i j k l m n o p q r s t u v w x y z

fire truck (noun)

A fire truck is a big truck that goes to put out big fires. Firefighters travel inside a fire truck.

A fire truck has big ladders on top of it.

fish (noun)

A fish is an animal that lives in water. It can breathe underwater. Fish have tails to help them swim.

Some people keep pet fish in a glass tank.

fist (noun)

Your fist is your hand with the fingers closed tightly together.

The angry man shook his fist at us.

flag (noun)

A flag is a piece of material with a colored pattern on it. Each country in the world has its own flag.

This is the flag of a country called France.

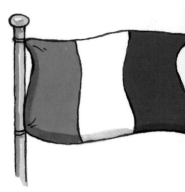

flame (noun)

When something burns it makes a flame. A flame is very hot so you should never touch it.

The match made an orange and red flame.

flat (adjective)

If something is flat it has no bumps in it. An area of flat land has no hills.

You can ride your bicycle fast on a flat road.

flower (noun)

A flower is a part of a plant. Lots of flowers are brightly colored and have a sweet smell.

You can give a bunch of flowers to someone you love.

fly (noun)

A fly is a small insect with two wings. It is not good to eat food if a fly has been on it.

There is a fly on my piece of strawberry pie!

fly (verb)

To fly is to move through the air. Airplanes and most birds can fly.

A kite will fly on a windy day.

foal (noun)

A foal is a baby horse.

A foal stays by its mother when it is first born.

foot (noun)

You have a foot at the end of each leg. The plural of foot is feet.

You have five toes on each foot.

forest (noun)

A forest is a piece of land where lots of trees grow.

In some forests the trees grow in straight lines.

a b c d e **f** g h i j k l m n o p q r s t u v w x y z

fork (noun)

A fork has sharp points on one end and a long handle. You use a small fork to eat your food.

You use a big fork to dig in the yard.

fox (noun)

A fox is a wild animal. A fox looks like a dog with a thick, furry tail.

A fox might look for food in your yard at night.

fossil (noun)

A fossil is found inside a rock. It is part of a plant or an animal that lived a very long time ago.

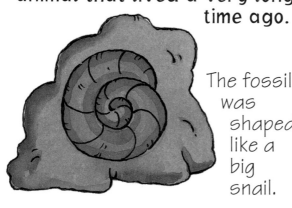

The fossil was shaped like a big snail.

friend (noun)

A friend is a person you like a lot. A friend is someone you know very well.

I sit next to my best friend at school.

fountain (noun)

A fountain shoots water up into the air. The water falls down and goes back inside it.

You may get wet if you stand very close to a fountain.

frog (noun)

A frog is a small animal that can live in or out of water. Frogs like to live in ponds.

A frog can jump a long way into the air.

a b c d e f g h i j k l m n o p q r s t u v w x y z

front (noun)
The front of something is the part that faces forward. Your eyes are in the front of your head.

A car has bright lights on the front.

fruit (noun)
A fruit grows on a bush or a tree. Apples, bananas, and oranges are fruits. Many fruits are juicy and good to eat.

Which of these fruits do you like to eat?

frost (noun)
Frost is ice that looks like powder. Frost comes when the weather is very cold.

The frost made patterns on the window.

full (adjective)
Something that is full has no space left inside it. You cannot put more into a full glass.

Your glass is full when the orange juice comes right to the top.

frown (verb)
If you frown you make your face have lines on it. People frown when they are angry, worried, or thinking hard.

My dad frowns when he is mad with me.

funny (adjective)
A funny thing or person makes you laugh.

My comic book has some funny stories in it.

a b c d e f g h i j k l m n o p q r s t u v w x y z

Gg

gallop (verb)

When a horse gallops it runs very fast.

The horse had to gallop to win the race.

game (noun)

A game is something that you play with other people. A game has rules that tell you what you can do.

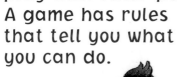

I played a game of tennis with my brother.

garage (noun)

A garage is a building where you keep your car.

Do you have a garage next to your home?

A garage is also a place where you take a car to be fixed. You can buy gas at some garages.

A garage has a special machine to lift cars off the floor.

garden (noun)
A garden is the land around a house. Trees, flowers, vegetables, and grass grow in a garden.

We grow rows of vegetables in our garden.

gate (noun)
A gate is a door in a fence or a wall. A gate can be made of wood or metal.

You can climb over some gates.

gaze (verb)
To gaze is to look at something for a long time. When you gaze you stare.

I often gaze at the stars out of my bedroom window.

gentle (adjective)
Gentle means quiet and kind. Someone who is gentle is not rough.

This mother is very gentle with her baby.

gerbil (noun)
A gerbil is a small, furry animal. It has long back legs and a long tail.

Many people keep a gerbil as a pet.

ghost (noun)
A ghost is not real. Some people think that a ghost is a person from long ago who comes back to visit us.

Some ghosts are friendly, but some are a little scary.

a b c d e f **g** h i j k l m n o p q r s t u v w x y z

giant (noun)

A giant is a very big person in a storybook. Giants are not real people.

This giant is even taller than a house.

girl (noun)

A girl is a female child. When a girl grows up she becomes a woman.

Lots of girls like to dance.

gift (noun)

A gift is something that you give to someone. It is a present.

I had lots of gifts to open on my birthday.

give (verb)

To give is to hand over something to someone else.

I like to give my mom some flowers for her birthday.

giraffe (noun)

A giraffe is an animal with a very long neck and tall, thin legs.

A giraffe can eat the leaves at the top of a tree.

glass (noun)

Glass is a hard material that you can see through. Windows and bottles are made from glass.

It is easy to break glass.

glasses (noun)
You wear glasses over your eyes to help you see better. Glasses have two pieces of glass or plastic inside a frame.

When you get older you may have to wear glasses to read.

glue (noun)
Glue is a thick, sticky liquid. You use glue to stick things together.

Chloe uses glue to stick the paper flowers onto the paper.

glove (noun)
You wear a glove on your hand. A glove has a part for each finger and for your **thumb**.

I wear my striped gloves when it is cold.

goat (noun)
A goat is a hairy animal with horns on its head. Some goats make milk.

A mommy goat is called a nanny. A daddy goat is called a billy.

glow (verb)
To glow is to give out a warm light.

The lights in our street glow in the dark.

gold (noun)
Gold is a shiny, yellow metal. It costs a lot of money. Gold is found in some kinds of rock.

Gold is used to make rings, bracelets, and earrings.

a b c d e f **g** h i j k l m n o p q r s t u v w x y z

goodbye (noun)
You say goodbye to someone when you leave. Sometimes you wave your hand when you say goodbye.

I wave goodbye to my grandma at the train station.

goose (noun)
A goose is a big bird with a long neck. A goose makes a very loud noise.

A goose will make a lot of noise if you go near it.

gorilla (noun)
A gorilla is a very big, strong animal. It has lots of hair on its body.

Gorillas live in the jungle in Africa.

grab (verb)
To grab is to take hold of something quickly.

Joe grabbed his bag and ran out of the door.

grandfather (noun)
A grandfather is the father of your mother or your father. Some people call their grandfather "grandad" or "grandpa."

My grandfather likes to play golf.

grandmother (noun)
A grandmother is the mother of your father or your mother. Some people call their grandmother "granny" or "grandma."

My mom and my grandmother look alike.

grape (noun)
A grape is a small, juicy fruit. You can eat grapes or use them to make juice or wine.

Grapes grow in bunches.

grow (verb)
To grow is to get bigger. Everything that is alive can grow.

The sunflowers in my yard grow taller every day.

grapefruit (noun)
A grapefruit is a big, round fruit with a thick skin. The inside of a grapefruit can be yellow, pink, or red.

You cut a grapefruit in half to eat it.

guinea pig (noun)
A guinea pig is a small, furry animal with no tail. You can keep guinea pigs as pets.

Guinea pigs like to eat lettuce and carrots.

grass (noun)
Grass is a green plant with very thin leaves. Animals such as cows and horses like to eat grass.

A lawn in the park is made up of grass.

guitar (noun)
A guitar is a musical instrument. It has strings that you play with your fingers.

I have a new, red guitar.

Hh

hair (noun)
Hair grows on your head and other parts of your body. It is made up of lots of soft, fine threads.

If you do not cut your hair it will grow very long.

hand (noun)
You have a hand at the end of each arm. Each hand has four fingers and a thumb.

You hold a bat and a ball in your hands.

half (noun)
When you cut something into two parts of the same size, each part is a half. You can also write a half as 1/2.

If you cut a pizza in two, you can eat one half each.

handle (noun)
A handle is the part of something you hold. You use the handle of a door to open and close the door.

My purse has two gray handles.

a b c d e f g h i j k l m n o p q r s t u v w x y z

hang (verb)
To hang something is to fasten the top part of it so it does not fall down.

At school I hang my coat on my hook.

happy (adjective)
Happy means not sad. You are pleased about things when you feel happy.

You are happy if you win a medal.

harbor (noun)
A harbor is a place where boats are kept safely. Harbors are usually near the ocean.

There are many sailboats in the harbor.

hard (adjective)
Hard means not soft. When you press a hard thing it does not change.

A stone bench is very hard.

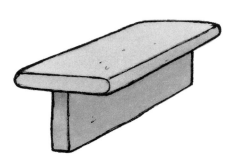

Hard also means not easy to do. If something is hard it is difficult.

It is hard to walk along a balance beam in the gym.

hare (noun)
A hare is an animal with very long ears. It is like a big rabbit. Hares can run very fast.

I saw a hare out in the field.

a b c d e f g h i j k l m n o p q r s t u v w x y z

hat (noun)

You wear a hat on top of your head. A hat keeps your head warm and dry.

There are many kinds of hats. Who does the red hat belong to?

hatch (verb)

To hatch means to come out of an egg when born. Baby birds, fishes, and snakes all hatch.

The chicks began to hatch out of their eggs.

hay (noun)

Hay is dry grass. Grass is cut and dried to make hay. You feed hay to animals such as horses and cows.

My horse likes to eat hay.

head (noun)

Your head is joined to your body. Your eyes, nose, and mouth are on your head.

Do you put a hat on your head when you go outside?

hear (verb)

You hear with your ears. You listen to sounds when you hear.

The children could hear the music on the radio.

heart (noun)

Your heart is in your chest at the top of your body. It is a very important part of you. Your heart pumps blood around your body.

When you run very fast you can feel your heart beating.

hedge (noun)
A hedge is a row of bushes that grow close together. A hedge often goes around a yard.

Birds often make their nest inside a hedge.

helmet (noun)
A helmet is a kind of hard hat. You wear it to protect your head.

The builder wears a yellow helmet when he works.

heel (noun)
Your heel is the back part of your foot.

Your heel is at one end of your foot, and your toes are at the other end.

help (verb)
To help is to do something useful for someone else.

I help my mom when she cooks.

helicopter (noun)
A helicopter is a machine that flies. It has blades on the top that spin around. Helicopters do not have wings.

A helicopter can fly straight up into the air.

hide (verb)
To hide is to put something in a place where no one can see it.

My sister hides her money in a pink box.

a b c d e f g h i j k l m n o p q r s t u v w x y z

high (adjective)
High is a long way up from the ground.

A hot air balloon goes very high in the sky.

hippopotamus (noun)
A hippopotamus is a very large animal. It has short legs. Hippopotamuses like to swim in muddy water.

A hippopotamus can open its mouth very wide.

hit (verb)
To hit is to touch something quickly and roughly.

You hit a tennis ball to make it go over the net.

hold (verb)
When you hold something you keep it in your hand. You hold something so that it does not fall.

I hold Dad's hand when I cross the road.

honey (noun)
Honey is a sweet, sticky food. It is made by bees inside a beehive.

Do you like to eat honey on bread?

horse (noun)
A horse is a large animal that can run fast. A baby horse is called a foal.

Have you ever had a ride on a horse?

hot (adjective)
Hot means not cold. When the sun shines you often feel hot.

If you eat very hot food you might burn your mouth.

hungry (adjective)
When you are hungry you want to eat food.

Do you feel hungry when it is lunchtime?

house (noun)
A house is a place where people live. It is usually made of stone, bricks, or wood.

Some houses have rooms on two or three stories.

hurry (verb)
To hurry is to go somewhere quickly.

Mom had to hurry to catch the train.

hug (verb)
To hug is to put your arms around someone or something. You usually hug someone that you like.

I like to hug my dad before I go to bed.

hutch (noun)
A hutch is a small house for animals. It is made of wood and wire. You keep pets such as rabbits and guinea pigs in a hutch.

My rabbit stays warm inside his hutch.

a b c d e f g **h** i j k l m n o p q r s t u v w x y z

ice (noun)
When water is very cold it turns into ice. Ice is cold and very hard.

You make ice cubes in a freezer.

icicle (noun)
An icicle is a long, thin piece of ice that hangs down. Icicles are made when water drips down in very cold weather.

Big icicles hang from our roof in the winter.

ice cream (noun)
Ice cream is a cold, sweet food. It is made from frozen cream and sugar.

What is your favorite kind of ice cream?

igloo (noun)
An igloo is a house made of ice and snow. The Inuit people from North America build igloos.

An igloo is made from big blocks of ice.

insect (noun)
An insect is a tiny animal with six legs.

Wasps, ants, and ladybugs are insects.

iron (noun)
An iron makes your clothes smooth and flat. You heat up an iron when you use it.

Never touch a hot iron, because it will burn you!

instrument (noun)
An instrument is something you play to make music. The piano, the trumpet, and the guitar are different instruments.

Can you play an instrument?

island (noun)
An island is a piece of land with water all around it.

You can travel all the way around an island in a boat.

invite (verb)
When you invite someone you ask that person to come to a party or to your home.

I'm going to invite my friends to a party.

ivy (noun)
Ivy is a shiny, green plant. It climbs up walls and along the ground.

Ivy grows up a wall very quickly.

a b c d e f g h i j k l m n o p q r s t u v w x y z

J j

jacket (noun)
A jacket is a short coat. Some jackets have a hood.

David puts on his bright blue jacket.

jaw (noun)
The jaw is the bony part of your mouth. Your teeth grow in your jaw. Many animals also have a jaw.

A crocodile has a very long jaw.

jar (noun)
A jar is made of glass or plastic. You keep foods and other things inside a jar.

You can buy strawberry jelly in a jar.

jeans (noun)
Jeans are a kind of pants. They are often made from a blue material.

Both boys and girls like to wear jeans.

jellyfish (noun)

A jellyfish is an animal that lives in the ocean. It has a soft, squishy body.

A jellyfish has lots of long, thin legs.

juggler (noun)

A juggler throws things in the air and then catches them. A juggler keeps lots of things moving in the air at the same time.

The juggler did a trick with eight balls.

jigsaw puzzle (noun)

A jigsaw puzzle is made of pieces of cardboard or wood. You put the pieces together to make a picture.

A jigsaw puzzle can have hundreds of different pieces.

juice (noun)

Juice is a drink made from fruits or vegetables. It often comes in cartons or bottles.

You can pour juice from a pitcher into your glass.

join (verb)

To join is to put two things together.

I can join these two pieces together.

jump (verb)

To jump is to leap into the air so that your feet do not touch the ground.

Do you like to jump on a trampoline?

a b c d e f g h i j k l m n o p q r s t u v w x y z

Kk

kangaroo (noun)
A kangaroo is an animal that lives in Australia. It has very strong back legs so it can hop very far.

A mommy kangaroo carries her baby in a special pocket called a pouch.

kennel (noun)
A kennel is a place that looks after dogs. Your dog goes to a kennel when you go away on vacation.

Our dog sleeps in a doghouse at the kennel.

keep (verb)
If you keep something you do not throw it away. You look after it for someone or for yourself.

I keep my bracelet inside a special box.

key (noun)
You use a key to open a door that is locked. Keys are usually made of metal.

You have to turn a key in the lock to open the door.

kick (verb)
When you kick a ball you hit it hard with your foot.

How far can you kick a soccer ball?

king (noun)
A king is a man who rules a country. A king is a very important person and is part of a royal family.

A king wears a crown on special days.

kid (noun)
A kid is a baby goat.

A kid can walk soon after it is born.

kiss (verb)
To kiss is to touch someone with your lips. You often kiss people because you are happy to see them.

I kiss my grandma when she comes to visit.

kind (adjective)
A kind person thinks of other people and helps them.

It is kind to give flowers to someone who is sick.

kitchen (noun)
A kitchen is a room in a home. You cook food and do the dishes in the kitchen.

Do you like to help in the kitchen?

kite (noun)
A kite is a toy that can fly in the air. It is connected to a very long piece of string.

Remember to hold the string tight when you fly your kite.

kneel (verb)
To kneel is to get down on your knees. When you kneel you have to bend your knees.

I kneel when I say my prayers at bedtime.

kitten (noun)
A kitten is a baby cat. A mother cat often has three or four kittens.

Our cat has four kittens.

knife (noun)
You use a knife to cut something. A knife has a handle and a blade that is sharp on one side.

A knife can be dangerous, so use it carefully.

knee (noun)
Your knee is part of your leg. It is where your leg bends.

Dancers have to bend their knees a lot.

koala (noun)
A koala is a furry animal that lives in Australia. It has a large, black nose and big, round ears.

Koalas live in trees and like to eat leaves.

Ll

label (noun)
A label is a small notice fixed to something. It shows useful information, such as the price or the size.

Look at the labels on these jars. What is in each jar?

ladder (noun)
A ladder is a set of steps. You use a ladder to get to high places.

The window cleaner has a long ladder.

lace (noun)
A lace is a long string that you can use to tie two things together.

Can you tie the laces on your shoes?

ladybug (noun)
A ladybug is a tiny insect that can fly. It is usually red with black spots.

How many spots can you count on this ladybug?

lake (noun)
A lake is an area of water with land all around it.

You can go rowing on this lake.

lamb (noun)
A lamb is a baby sheep. Lambs live on farms.

Lambs like to skip and play.

lamp (noun)
A lamp gives off light. You can switch a lamp on and off.

Do you have a lamp next to your bed?

land (noun)
The land is the part of the world not covered by ocean.

A map shows the shape of the land and the ocean.

large (adjective)
Large means that something is big. It is the opposite of small.

An elephant is a large animal.

late (adjective)
You are late when you arrive somewhere after the time you are expected.

You may have to run if you are very late.

laugh (verb)
To laugh is to make a sound that shows you are happy.

Clowns make you laugh because they do funny things.

leaf (noun)
A leaf is the flat, green part of a plant. Some trees lose their leaves in fall and grow new ones in spring.

The leaf on an oak tree is bright green.

lawn (noun)
A lawn is an area of short grass. A yard often has a tidy, green lawn.

You step on stones to walk across this lawn.

learn (verb)
To learn is to find out about something that you did not know before.

Young children learn to write when they go to school.

lazy (adjective)
If you are lazy you do not want to work or do any exercise.

If you feel lazy you might get up late in the morning.

leave (verb)
To leave is to go away.

People wave goodbye when they leave.

a b c d e f g h i j k **l** m n o p q r s t u v w x y z

left (adjective)
Left is the opposite side to right. You have a left hand and a right hand.

Katie holds up her left hand.

leg (noun)
Your leg joins your body to your feet. You use your legs to walk, run, and climb.

You have two legs, but many animals have four legs.

lemon (noun)
A lemon is a very sour, yellow fruit. Lemons grow on trees in hot countries.

You use lemons to make a drink called lemonade.

leopard (noun)
A leopard is a kind of large, wild cat. It has black spots and sharp teeth and claws.

The leopard is sitting in a tree.

letter (noun)
You use letters to make words. There are 26 different letters. Together they make up the alphabet.

You use the letter "j" to start the word "jump."

A letter is also a piece of paper with words on it. You send a message in a letter.

You usually put a letter inside an envelope.

lift (verb)
When you lift something you pick it up with your hands.

This box is very heavy to lift.

lion (noun)
A lion is a large, fierce animal that lives in Africa. Lions are a kind of wild cat.

Lions are not friendly animals.

light (adjective)
When it is light you can see what is around you. Light means not dark.

Is it light outside when you wake up in the morning?

lip (noun)
Your lip is the soft, red part around your mouth. You move your lips when you speak.

My sister puts pink lipstick on her lips.

light (noun)
A light helps you to see in the dark. Some lights have electric bulbs in them.

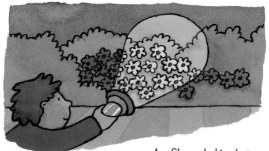

A flashlight shines a light in the dark.

list (noun)
To make a list you write things down one after the other.

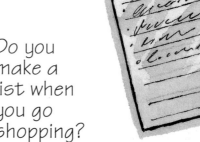

Do you make a list when you go shopping?

a b c d e f g h i j k **l** m n o p q r s t u v w x y z

little (noun)
Something is little when it is not big. Little means the same as small.

A sweater that is too little does not fit very well.

lock (verb)
If you lock something, you fasten it shut with a key.

When you lock a door you need a key to open it.

live (verb)
You live in your home. You live in the place where you eat and sleep.

Who do you live with?

log (noun)
A log is a thick piece of wood. It has been cut from a tree.

A log burns well in a fireplace.

lizard (noun)
A lizard is a small animal with a long tail and four short legs.

Some lizards look like tiny crocodiles, but they will not hurt you.

long (adjective)
Long means not short. A giraffe uses its long neck to eat the leaves at the top of trees.

If your hair is very long it will go past your shoulders.

look (verb)
You use your eyes to look at things.

A pirate may look for ships to attack.

love (verb)
To love someone or something is to like that person or thing a lot.

I love my cat very much.

lose (verb)
If you lose something you cannot find it.

If you lose a button you can't close your shirt.

low (adjective)
Low means near the ground. If something is low it is not high up.

The wall around the fountain is very low.

loud (adjective)
A loud noise is easy to hear. If you play a drum you make a loud sound.

Do you put your fingers over your ears when you hear a loud noise?

lucky (adjective)
If you are lucky things seem to go right for you. A lucky person might win things.

A gold horseshoe is my lucky charm.

a b c d e f g h i j k **l** m n o p q r s t u v w x y z

Mm

machine (noun)
A machine has moving parts that make it work. Machines help us to do jobs more quickly.

A hairdryer is a handy machine.

magic (noun)
Magic makes something impossible happen in a story.

The fairy used her wand to make magic.

magazine (noun)
A magazine is a thin book with lots of pictures and stories in it.

You can buy a magazine at a newspaper stand.

magician (noun)
A magician is a person who does clever tricks. Magicians do magic for us.

Some magicians can make a rabbit come out of a hat.

magnet (noun)
A magnet is a special piece of metal. It pulls iron and steel things toward it.

A magnet can pick up paperclips.

make (verb)
You make something when you put lots of things together.

Do you like to make things with blocks?

male (noun)
A male is a man or a boy. Male is the opposite of female.

A father is a male.

mammal (noun)
A mammal is an animal that feeds its babies with its own milk.

A pig is a mammal that has lots of babies at once.

man (noun)
A man is a grown-up boy.

A man can grow a beard.

mane (noun)
A mane is the long hair that grows along the neck of a horse or a lion.

I comb my horse's mane to make her look pretty.

abcdefghijklmnopqrstuvwxyz

map (noun)

A map is a drawing that shows you where places are. Some maps show you how to get to another city.

This map shows you some land with an ocean around it.

mask (noun)

You wear a mask over your face. It protects your face or makes you look different.

Have you ever worn a mask at a party?

marble (noun)

A marble is a little, glass ball. You play a game by rolling marbles along the ground.

Marbles are made in pretty colors.

mast (noun)

A mast is a tall piece of wood on a sailing boat. It holds up the sails.

Long ago, sailing boats used to have three masts.

march (verb)

To march means to walk with quick steps, like a soldier.

The toy soldiers march across the table.

match (noun)

A match is a small stick that makes a flame. You rub the thick end on something rough.

You should never, ever play with matches!

maze (noun)

A maze is a big puzzle with lots of paths inside it. It is difficult to find your way out of a maze.

Sometimes mazes are made out of tall hedges.

measure (verb)

To measure is to find out how big or how heavy something is.

You can measure yourself with a height chart.

meal (noun)

A meal is the food you eat at certain times of the day. Breakfast and dinner are meals.

Which is your favorite meal of the day?

medal (noun)

A medal is a small circle of shiny metal. You might get a medal if you win a race or do something brave.

This shiny medal hangs around your neck.

mean (adjective)

If you are mean you are nasty to someone or you do not like sharing things.

Laughing at somebody who is hurt is mean.

medicine (noun)

You take medicine when you feel sick. It is the liquid or the pills that you swallow.

Medicine will help to make you feel better.

medium (adjective)
Medium means in the middle. It is between big and small.

If you are not very tall or very short, you are medium height.

meet (verb)
When you meet someone you go to the same place at the same time to see that person.

Where do you meet your best friend?

melon (noun)
A melon is a large, juicy fruit. It has a thick, yellow or green skin.

You cut a melon into slices to eat it.

melt (verb)
When something melts it changes to a liquid. Heat makes things melt.

Your popsicle will melt on a sunny day.

mermaid (noun)
A mermaid is a woman in a storybook who has a tail like a fish.

In stories, mermaids often comb their hair.

message (noun)
A message is the words you send to others when you cannot see them or talk to them.

You can write a message or send it on a computer.

metal (noun)

A metal is a hard and strong material. Gold and silver are metals.

This knife and fork are made of metal.

middle (noun)

The middle of something is halfway between its two sides. The middle is also the center of something.

The arrow is in the middle of the target.

milk (noun)

Milk is a white liquid that comes from some animals. Cows, goats, and many other animals feed milk to their babies.

Babies like to drink lots of milk.

mirror (noun)

A mirror is a special piece of glass. You can see yourself in a mirror.

You can look in a mirror and wave at yourself.

miss (verb)

If you miss something you do not catch it or hit it.

The soccer player might miss a goal.

mistake (noun)

A mistake is something that is wrong.

The teacher marked the mistake with a big, red X.

a b c d e f g h i j k l m n o p q r s t u v w x y z

mix (verb)
If you mix things, you stir them together.

You can mix blue and red paints to make purple.

monkey (noun)
A monkey is a wild animal with long arms and legs. Monkeys live in hot places.

A monkey uses its hands and feet to climb in the trees.

moat (noun)
A moat is a ditch around a castle. A moat is usually filled with water.

The moat stopped the enemy soldiers from attacking the castle.

monster (noun)
A monster is a big, scary creature in a storybook.

Can you draw a funny monster?

money (noun)
Money is metal coins or pieces of paper. You need money to buy things.

Do you keep your money in a change purse?

month (noun)
Every year has twelve months in it. Each month has a name.

In which month is your birthday?

moon (noun)
The moon shines in the sky at night. It moves slowly around the Earth.

The moon is not always the same shape each night.

moss (noun)
Moss is a flat, green plant. It grows on trees and rocks and in damp places. Moss has no flowers.

There is lots of moss on the branch of this tree.

mop (noun)
A mop is a long handle with a sponge or pieces of string at one end. You use a mop to wash a floor.

You use a mop with a pail of water.

moth (noun)
A moth is an insect that looks like a butterfly. Moths fly around at night.

A moth is not as brightly colored as a butterfly.

morning (noun)
Morning is the first half of the day. It ends at 12 o'clock in the middle of the day.

Children go to school in the morning.

mother (noun)
A mother is a woman who has a child or children.

My mother likes to play with our new baby.

a b c d e f g h i j k l **m** n o p q r s t u v w x y z

motorcycle (noun)

A motorcycle has two wheels and an engine. Two people can ride on a motorcycle.

A racing motorcycle drives fast around a track.

mountain (noun)

A mountain is a very high hill. Mountains are hard to climb.

Sometimes there is snow on the top of a mountain.

mouse (noun)

A mouse is a small, furry animal with a long tail. Mice can live outside or in your home.

A mouse can make its nest in a field of grain.

mouth (noun)

Your mouth is the part of your face that you use for talking and eating.

You use your mouth when you whistle.

move (verb)

To move is to go from one place to another.

When you walk along you move.

mow (verb)

To mow is to cut grass when it grows too long.

You can sit on a machine to mow the grass.

mud (noun)

Mud is wet soil. It is a mixture of earth and water.

When it rains you get mud all over your boots.

mushroom (noun)

A mushroom is a small living thing that looks like a tiny umbrella. You can eat some mushrooms.

It is not safe to eat mushrooms that grow in the woods.

mug (noun)

A mug is a big cup. It does not have a saucer. People often drink coffee or hot chocolate out of mugs.

Some mugs have pictures or writing on the outside.

muscle (noun)

A muscle is a part inside your body. You use your muscles to help you move. You have lots of different muscles.

If you do exercises your muscles will become stronger.

multiply (verb)

To multiply is to do a sum to make a number bigger. If you multiply a number by two, the number is twice as big.

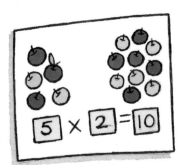

$5 \times 2 = 10$

If you multiply five apples by 2, the answer is 10 apples.

music (noun)

Music is the sound you make when you sing or play an instrument.

The violinist played beautiful music.

Nn

nail (noun)

A nail is a thin piece of metal with a point at one end. You use nails to attach together pieces of wood.

Dad hammers the nail into the wood.

A nail is also the hard part at the end of each of your fingers and toes.

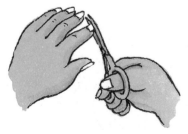

You need to cut your nails often because they grow.

name (noun)

Your name is what you are called. A name is the word you use to talk about someone or something.

My name is Anna!

Anna

narrow (adjective)

Narrow means not very wide. If something is narrow it is not far from one side to the other.

I live on a very narrow street.

naughty (adjective)

If someone is naughty that person does not behave well. Naughty people do not do what they are told.

The naughty puppy chewed my teddy bear.

neck (noun)

Your neck is the part of your body between your head and your shoulders.

Lauren wears red beads around her neck.

necklace (noun)

A necklace is a row of beads or a chain that you wear around your neck.

My favorite necklace is made of blue and silver beads.

needle (noun)

A needle is a very thin piece of metal for sewing. It has a sharp point at one end and a hole at the other end.

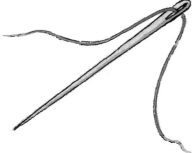

This needle has blue thread in it.

neighbor (noun)

A neighbor is a person who lives next door to you or near you.

I talk to my neighbor over the fence.

nest (noun)

A nest is a home that birds and mice build. They build nests with twigs, grass, and leaves.

Baby birds stay in a nest until they can fly.

a b c d e f g h i j k l m **n** o p q r s t u v w x y z

net (noun)
A net has a long handle and a soft basket made from string. You use a net to catch fish.

Do you take a net when you go to the beach?

new (adjective)
New means not old. New things have never been used or worn.

New sneakers always look very shiny and clean.

newspaper (noun)
A newspaper has big pieces of paper that are folded in half. Writing and pictures are printed on the paper.

A newspaper tells you what is happening around the world.

next (adjective)
Next is the one that comes after this one.

The next day after Monday is Tuesday.

night (noun)
Night is the time between the evening and the morning. Night is when it is dark outside.

Owls fly around during the night.

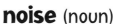

noise (noun)
A noise is a sound you hear. If a noise is loud, you try to find out what it is.

An airplane makes a loud noise.

noon (noun)
Noon is the middle of the day. The time at noon is 12 o'clock.

I eat my lunch at noon.

number (noun)
A number tells you how many of something you have. You use numbers to count.

Can you see the number 5 in this picture?

nose (noun)
Your nose is on your face. You breathe through it. You also smell with your nose.

You use your nose to find out if something smells good.

nurse (noun)
A nurse looks after people who are sick. Most nurses work in hospitals.

Many nurses wear white shoes at work.

note (noun)
A note is a short letter that you write to someone.

I wrote a note to say thank you for my gift.

nut (noun)
A nut is a fruit with a hard shell. You take off the shell and eat the nut inside.

It is easy to take the shells off these nuts.

a b c d e f g h i j k l m **n** o p q r s t u v w x y z

Oo

oar (noun)

An oar is a long pole made from wood. It has a flat part at one end. You use oars to make a rowboat move on water.

You need two oars when you row a boat.

oats (noun)

Oats are the tiny seeds of a cereal plant. Farmers grow oats to feed their animals.

You use oats to make oatmeal.

obey (verb)

If you obey someone you do what that person tells you to do.

The sheepdog obeyed the farmer and sat down.

ocean (noun)

An ocean is a large area of water. It is a very big sea.

You can look at the ocean when you stand on the beach.

a b c d e f g h i j k l m n o p q r s t u v w x y z

octopus (noun)

An octopus is an animal that lives in the ocean. It has a soft body and eight arms.

An octopus uses its arms to swim through the water.

odd (adjective)

Odd means strange or different.

My grandma wears very odd shoes.

office (noun)

An office is a place where people go to work. In an office you sit at a desk to work.

People are busy on the telephone in this office.

oil (noun)

Oil is a thick, black liquid. It is found under the ground or under the ocean. Oil helps to make machines work.

The oil spilled onto the beach.

old (adjective)

Old is not new. Things that people keep for a long time are old.

Old sneakers are not as shiny as new ones.

Someone who is old has been alive for a long time. An old person is not young.

The old king had a long, gray beard.

omelette (noun)

An omelette is a food you eat. To make an omelette you mix together eggs and milk and then fry them.

I had a cheese and tomato omelette for my dinner.

open (adjective)

Open means not shut. When a window is open the rain may come into your house.

If the front door is open you can walk into the house.

opposite (noun)

An opposite is something that is very different from another thing. Hot is the opposite of cold.

Straight is the opposite of squiggly.

orange (noun)

An orange is a round, juicy fruit. You take off the thick, orange skin and eat the juicy part inside.

Oranges keep you healthy, so they are good to eat.

orchard (noun)

An orchard is a place where fruit trees grow.

There are lots of apple trees in the orchard.

owl (noun)

An owl is a bird with big, round eyes. It looks for food at night and catches mice, frogs, and insects to eat.

An owl makes a loud hooting sound at night.

Pp

package (noun)
A package is a small parcel.

The package had red string around it.

padlock (noun)
A padlock is a small, metal lock. You can use it to lock gates and closets.

You need a key to open this padlock.

paddle (verb)
To paddle is to walk about in water that is not very deep.

Michael likes to paddle at the edge of the ocean.

page (noun)
A piece of paper in a book is called a page. You turn the page when you are reading.

How many pages are in this dictionary?

a b c d e f g h i j k l m n o **p** q r s t u v w x y z

paint (noun)

Paint is a colored liquid. You use paints and a brush to make a picture.

What colors are the paints in this picture?

paint (verb)

To paint is to put colors on a piece of paper or on walls.

You use a big brush to paint the walls of a room.

pair (noun)

A pair is two things that go together. You use a pair at the same time.

Martha is wearing a pair of red shoes.

palm (noun)

A palm is a tree that grows in hot places. Palm trees have long leaves that grow at the top of the tree.

A palm tree has a long, thin trunk.

Your palm is also the inside part of your hand.

Your palm has lots of lines on it.

pancake (noun)

A pancake is a thin, flat food. It is made from eggs, flour, and milk that you mix together and cook.

Do you like syrup on your pancake?

panda (noun)
A panda is a very large, black and white, furry animal. Pandas live in China.

There are not many left in the world.

Pandas love to eat bamboo shoots.

parachute (noun)
A parachute is a big piece of cloth. It helps a person fall slowly through the air.

A person who jumps out of a plane wears a parachute.

pane (noun)
A pane is a sheet of glass in a window.

This window has four panes of glass.

parcel (noun)
A parcel is something that is wrapped in paper. You usually send a parcel in the mail.

What do you think is inside this parcel?

paper (noun)
Paper is the material you use to write on. You can also paint on paper and use it to wrap things.

You can buy pretty paper to wrap up a present.

parent (noun)
A parent is a person who has a child. Your mother and your father are your parents.

My parents wave goodbye at the school gate.

park (noun)

A park is a large area where people can walk and play. It has trees and flowers, and sometimes a playground.

Is there a park near your home?

parrot (noun)

A parrot is a bird with very bright feathers. Parrots usually live in warm countries.

You can teach some pet parrots to say words.

party (noun)

A party is a group of people who are having fun together.

Your friends come to a party on your birthday.

pass (verb)

To pass something is to hand it to another person.

I pass the pitcher to my sister.

passenger (noun)

A passenger is someone who travels in a car, a bus, a train, a boat, or an airplane.

The passengers wait to get on the bus.

passport (noun)

A passport is a little book with your name and your photograph in it. You need your passport when you visit another country.

Do you have a passport?

pasta (noun)
Pasta is a food that comes in lots of shapes. It is made from flour, eggs, and water. You boil it to make it soft.

Which is your favorite kind of pasta?

pea (noun)
A pea is a small, green vegetable. Peas are round and they grow inside long, thin pods.

You can eat peas uncooked or you can cook them.

paw (noun)
A paw is the foot of an animal. Some paws have sharp claws at the front.

Our cat likes to lick her paw.

peach (noun)
A peach is a round, juicy fruit. It has a soft skin and a big pit in the middle.

Peaches can have red or yellow skins.

pay (verb)
To pay is to give money for something. You pay when you buy something from a store.

You pay for a ticket at the movie theater.

peacock (noun)
A peacock is a large bird with beautiful feathers. A peacock cannot fly.

A peacock can spread out the feathers in its tail.

a b c d e f g h i j k l m n o **p** q r s t u v w x y z

peanut (noun)

A peanut is a small nut that grows under the ground. It has a soft shell.

Peanut butter is made from peanuts.

pebble (noun)

A pebble is a small, smooth stone. You can find pebbles on the beach or in the bottom of rivers and streams.

When you touch a pebble it is smooth and round.

pear (noun)

A pear is a juicy fruit. It has a green or yellow skin. Pears have small brown seeds in the middle.

The inside of a pear is almost white.

pedal (noun)

A pedal is a part on a bicycle. You push on the pedals with your feet to make the bicycle move.

You push hard on the pedals to go uphill.

pearl (noun)

A pearl is a small, round stone. Some pearls are grown in shells. Others are made in factories.

Pearls can be white, cream, pink, or black.

peel (verb)

If you peel a fruit or a vegetable, you take the skin off it.

Mom uses a knife to peel my apple.

peep (verb)
To peep is to take a quick look at something.

The dancer tried to peep through the curtains.

pencil (noun)
A pencil is a thin stick with black or colored material inside it. You use a pencil to write and draw.

You can use a pencil to write a letter.

pelican (noun)
A pelican is a large water bird. It has a big pouch like a bag under its beak.

The pelican has a fish in its pouch.

penguin (noun)
A penguin is a black and white bird that lives near the ocean.

Penguins cannot fly, but they can dive and swim.

Most penguins live in very cold places.

pen (noun)
You use a pen to write words. A pen has ink inside it.

I use a pen to write in my diary.

pepper (noun)
Pepper is a powder with a hot taste. You sprinkle it over food to make it taste stronger.

You keep pepper in a pepper shaker.

a b c d e f g h i j k l m n o p q r s t u v w x y z

abcdefghijklmnopqrstuvwxyz

perform (verb)
If you perform, you act, sing, or dance in front of a lot of people.

The children perform their school play.

person (noun)
Every man, woman, or child is a person.

My teacher is my favorite person.

perfume (noun)
Perfume is a liquid with a sweet smell. You put perfume on your face and body so that you smell nice.

You can make perfume from flower petals.

pet (noun)
A pet is an animal that you keep at home. You usually love a pet and like to look after it.

My two pets are a dog and a rabbit.

permit (verb)
If someone permits you to do something, that person allows you to do it.

The soldier permits us to cross the bridge.

petal (noun)
A petal is part of a flower. Petals are usually colorful and they often smell sweet.

A daisy has lots of little, white petals.

photograph (noun)

A photograph is a picture that you take with a camera.

Here is a photograph of my sister on the beach.

pick (verb)

To pick is to pull off part of a plant. You pick apples off a tree.

I like to pick flowers from our yard.

piano (noun)

A piano is a large musical instrument. It has black and white pieces called keys. You press the keys with your fingers to make music.

You sit on a stool when you play the piano.

picture (noun)

A picture is a drawing, a painting, or a photograph.

You can hang a picture on the wall.

picnic (noun)

A picnic is a meal that you carry with you. You eat a picnic outside.

We had a picnic on the grass.

pie (noun)

A pie has pastry on the outside and cream or fruit in the middle. You bake a pie in the oven.

Which is your favorite pie?

a b c d e f g h i j k l m n o **p** q r s t u v w x y z

piece (noun)

A piece is a part of something. If you cut off a slice of cake you have a piece.

I had the last piece of the puzzle in my hand.

pig (noun)

A pig is a farm animal with a curly tail and short legs. A baby pig is called a piglet.

Many pigs are pink, but some are brown or black.

pigeon (noun)

A pigeon is a large, gray bird. It has a small head and a round body.

You often see pigeons in the middle of cities.

pigpen (noun)

A pigpen is a place where pigs live on the farm. A farmer keeps his pigs in a pigpen.

A pigpen is usually very muddy.

pile (noun)

A pile is a lot of things that are placed on top of each other.

The waitress carried a big pile of plates.

pill (noun)

A pill is a small, round tablet that contains medicine. You might have to take a pill if you are sick.

You can swallow a pill with a glass of water.

pillar (noun)
A pillar is a post that helps to hold up a building. Pillars are usually made of wood or stone.

The roof was held up by four pillars.

pin (noun)
A pin is a small, thin piece of metal. It is very sharp at one end.

A pin holds pieces of material together.

pillow (noun)
A pillow is a cloth case filled with soft material. You put your head on a pillow when you sleep.

Our cat likes to sleep on my pillow.

pinch (verb)
If you pinch you squeeze something between your thumb and your finger.

Joshua tried to pinch his brother's arm.

pilot (noun)
A pilot is a person who flies an airplane. Most pilots wear a uniform.

A pilot has to fly the airplane safely.

pineapple (noun)
A pineapple is a yellow fruit. The skin is hard and prickly, but the inside is juicy and sweet.

You cut off the skin before you eat a pineapple.

pipe (noun)

A pipe is a long, empty tube. It is made of plastic or metal. Gas or liquid moves through pipes.

A pipe carries fresh water to drink.

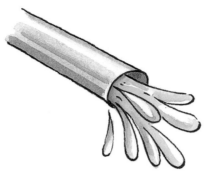

pizza (noun)

Pizza is a food with a bread crust at the bottom. It has different things on the top, such as cheese or pepperoni.

Do you like cheese and tomato pizza?

pirate (noun)

A pirate is a robber who steals things from ships.

The pirate wore a big, black hat.

plain (adjective)

If something is plain it has no decoration on it.

Jennifer wore a plain, blue skirt.

pitcher (noun)

A pitcher is a container for liquids. It has an open top and a handle.

A pitcher has a spout to make it easy to pour.

planet (noun)

A planet is a big, round object that moves around in space. We live on the planet Earth.

The planet called Mars is a red color.

plant (noun)
A plant is any living thing that is not an animal. Trees, bushes, and garden flowers are plants.

A plant needs sunshine and water to grow.

plant (verb)
To plant is to put seeds or plants into the ground to grow.

I planted a pack of sunflower seeds.

plastic (noun)
Plastic is a strong material that is used to make many different things.

Spoons, umbrellas, toys, and pails can be made of plastic.

plate (noun)
A plate is flat and round. You eat food from it. Plates come in many different sizes.

Some plates have bright colors and patterns on them.

platform (noun)
A platform is the place in a railway station where you wait for a train.

We waited on the platform for the next train to Chicago.

play (verb)
To play is to have fun with your friends or with your toys.

My little sister likes to play in the sandbox.

playground (noun)
A playground is a place outdoors where children can play.

Our new playground has a slide and swings.

plum (noun)
A plum is a small, juicy fruit. It has a pit in the middle. Plums can be red, green, or yellow.

We picked a basket of plums.

pocket (noun)
A pocket is a small bag that is sewn into your clothes. Not everything you wear has a pocket.

My dad said he had nothing in his pockets.

point (noun)
A point is the sharp end of something. A needle has a point at one end.

Mom pricked her finger on the point of a needle!

point (verb)
When you point at something you use your finger to show where it is.

Daniel tried to point to his favorite comic book.

polar bear (noun)
A polar bear is a very big, white bear. Its body is covered with thick fur. Polar bears live in cold places.

A polar bear makes holes in the ice.

pole (noun)
A pole is a long, round stick. It can be made from wood, metal, or plastic.

There is a wooden pole in the middle of our tent.

pony (noun)
A pony is a kind of horse. A pony is small even when it is fully grown.

I like to ride my pony every day.

police officer (noun)
A police officer is someone who protects people and things. Police officers make sure that people behave.

The police officer directs the traffic in the street.

pool (noun)
A pool is a small area of water. The water in a pool does not move very much.

There was a pool of muddy water on the street.

pond (noun)
A pond is a small area of water with land all around it. It is not as big as a lake.

We have frogs in the pond in our yard.

poor (adjective)
If you are poor you do not have much money. Poor means not rich.

Long ago, some poor people did not wear shoes.

a b c d e f g h i j k l m n o **p** q r s t u v w x y z

popcorn (noun)
Popcorn is a snack food. It is made from corn that grows big and soft when you cook it.

I eat popcorn when I go to the movies.

poppy (noun)
A poppy is a brightly colored flower. Many kinds of poppy are red.

Wild poppies grow in the field.

porch (noun)
A porch is a little area with a roof at the front of a house. A porch is in front of a door.

You can stay dry in a porch when it rains.

porcupine (noun)
A porcupine is a small animal with long, sharp hairs on its back. A porcupine's spiky hairs are called quills.

The porcupine uses its quills to scare other animals.

portrait (noun)
A portrait is a picture of someone. A portrait can be a drawing, a painting, or a photograph.

There was a large portrait of the queen on the wall.

post (noun)
A post is a strong, straight piece of wood. You place a post in the ground.

The gate is attached to two thick posts.

postcard (noun)
A postcard is a piece of card with a picture on it. You write a message on the back and send it to someone.

I sent a postcard from New York.

poster (noun)
A poster is a large picture or announcement. You can put it on a wall or a bulletin board.

My sister has lots of posters in her bedroom.

potato (noun)
A potato is a vegetable that grows under the ground. It has a red or brown skin and is white on the inside.

You make French fries and potato chips from potatoes.

pouch (noun)
A pouch is a pocket of skin on some animals. Mommy kangaroos have a pouch on their front.

A baby kangaroo grows in its mother's pouch.

pour (verb)
To pour is to make liquid flow out of a bottle or a pitcher into something else.

She started to pour the milk into her glass.

practice (verb)
To practice is to keep doing something lots of times until you get better at it.

Tom practices the piano every afternoon.

a b c d e f g h i j k l m n o **p** q r s t u v w x y z

present (noun)
You give a present to someone on a special day. A present is usually wrapped in pretty paper.

Do you get lots of presents on your birthday?

princess (noun)
A princess is the daughter of a king or a queen. A princess can also be the wife of a prince.

The princess wore a beautiful, pink dress.

prick (verb)
To prick is to make a small hole with something that is sharp.

My mom sometimes pricks her finger on a rose.

prize (noun)
A prize is something that you give to a person who wins a race or a competition.

The first prize was a large trophy.

prince (noun)
A prince is the son of a king or a queen.

In fairy tales, a prince often rides a white horse.

promise (verb)
If you promise to do something, you say that you will definitely do it.

I promise to help do the dishes each day.

propeller (noun)

A propeller is part of a ship or an airplane. The propeller spins round to make the ship or plane move.

This propeller is on the front of a small airplane.

pull (verb)

To pull is to take hold of something and move it toward you.

I tried very hard to pull the rope.

puddle (noun)

A puddle is a little pool of water. There are lots of puddles when it rains.

You need to wear boots if you want to splash in puddles.

pump (noun)

A pump is a machine that pushes air or liquid in or out of something. You use a pump to put air in your bicycle tires.

Do you have a pump like this for your bicycle?

puffin (noun)

A puffin is a black and white bird that lives by the ocean. It has a big blue and orange beak.

A puffin likes to eat lots of fish.

pumpkin (noun)

A pumpkin is a large fruit with an orange skin. Some people like to eat pumpkin pie.

People carve faces on pumpkins at Halloween.

a b c d e f g h i j k l m n o **p** q r s t u v w x y z

puppet (noun)

A puppet is a toy that you can move. Some puppets have strings. Some are like a glove that you wear.

You can make this puppet walk, run, and dance.

put (verb)

To put something is to place it or move it.

Dad put the books on the desk.

puppy (noun)

A puppy is a young dog.

A puppy likes to play with other puppies.

pyramid (noun)

A pyramid is a building that goes up to a point. It does not have a roof.

Each side of a pyramid is shaped like a triangle.

push (verb)

To push is to move something away from you.

I help Mom to push our baby's stroller.

python (noun)

A python is a very strong and large snake. It lives in the jungle and is very dangerous.

This python lives in a tree.

Qq

quack (verb)
When a duck quacks it makes a loud noise.

Ducks quack loudly when you get too close to them.

quarrel (verb)
If you quarrel you do not agree with another person. People often get angry when they quarrel.

My brother and I quarreled over our kite.

quarter (noun)
When you divide something into four equal parts, each part is a quarter.

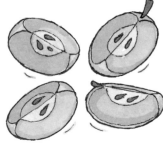

Do you cut your apple into quarters?

A quarter is also a coin. It is worth 25 cents, or one quarter of a dollar.

A US quarter has a picture of an eagle on the back.

a b c d e f g h i j k l m n o p q r s t u v w x y z

queen (noun)

A queen is a woman who is the head of a country. A queen can also be the wife of a king.

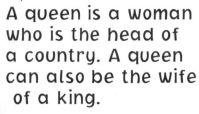

On special days a queen wears a crown on her head.

quiet (adjective)

If you are quiet you make no noise or only a tiny noise. Quiet means not loud.

Shhh! You have to be quiet when a baby is asleep.

question (noun)

You ask a question when you want to find out about something. "What time is it?" is a question.

Why?

Children ask a lot of questions that begin with the word "Why?"

quilt (noun)

A quilt is a soft covering for a bed. It is made of squares of cloth.

The quilt on my bed has lots of colors in it.

quick (adjective)

If you are quick, you do something fast. Quick means not slow.

A quick runner will often win a race.

quiz (noun)

A quiz is a game where people answer lots of questions. The person who gets the most answers correct is the winner.

You can often watch a quiz show on the television.

Rr

rabbit (noun)
A rabbit is a small, furry animal with long ears. Most rabbits are wild but some are pets.

Rabbits like to eat lots of lettuce.

race car (noun)
A race car is a very fast car. It drives around a special race track.

Race cars are faster than ordinary cars.

race (noun)
A race is a competition to see who is the fastest at something. Horses, cars, and people all take part in races.

The winner of a race reaches the finish line first.

racket (noun)
A racket is a bat with strings that are stretched across it tightly. You use a racket to play some sports.

Joanna holds her tennis racket in her left hand.

radiator (noun)

A radiator makes a room warm. A radiator is made of metal and is full of hot water. It is fixed to a wall.

The room is warm because the radiator is on.

radio (noun)

You listen to music and talking on the radio. A radio is a small machine made of metal or plastic.

I listen to my favorite music on the radio.

rain (noun)

Rain is drops of water that fall from the sky. Rain comes from the clouds.

If you are outside in the rain you will get wet.

rainbow (noun)

A rainbow is a thick arch of different colors. You see it in the sky when the sun shines and it rains at the same time.

A rainbow has seven colors. Can you name all of them?

rake (noun)

A rake is a garden tool with a long handle. It has a row of spikes at one end.

You use a rake to clear up dead leaves.

raspberry (noun)

A raspberry is a small, red fruit. Raspberries grow on bushes.

A raspberry is very juicy and good to eat.

rat (noun)
A rat is an animal that looks like a large mouse. Most rats are brown or black. Some people keep rats as pets.

Rats often live in cities and towns.

rattle (noun)
A rattle is a small toy for a baby. It makes a noise when you shake it.

I bought a rattle for the new baby.

reach (verb)
To reach is to stretch out your hand to get something.

You must reach up to get something from a high shelf.

reach (verb)
To reach a place means to arrive there.

The hikers were happy to reach the bridge.

read (verb)
To read is to look at words and know what they mean.

Do you like to sit in a big chair when you read a story?

receipt (noun)
A receipt is a piece of paper that tells you how much money you have paid for something.

She gave me a receipt for my new books.

a b c d e f g h i j k l m n o p q r s t u v w x y z

recipe (noun)
A recipe tells you how to cook something to eat. You follow the instructions in a recipe.

A cookbook is full of recipes.

reed (noun)
A reed is a tall grass plant. It has a long, thin stem. Reeds grow beside lakes and rivers.

Ducks sometimes hide among the reeds.

recorder (noun)
A recorder is a musical instrument that you blow. It has holes that you cover up with your fingers to make different sounds.

Do you know what a recorder sounds like?

refrigerator (noun)
A refrigerator is a machine that keeps food cold. It is like a metal cabinet and has a motor. We sometimes call it a fridge for short.

Food stays fresh and cool inside a refrigerator.

recycle (verb)
When you recycle something you make something new out of something old.

You can recycle glass bottles.

reindeer (noun)
A reindeer is a big deer with horns. It lives in cold countries.

Here is Santa Claus with his reindeer Rudolph.

remember (verb)
To remember is to think of something and not forget it.

Do you remember to brush your teeth every day?

reptile (noun)
A reptile is an animal with a scaly skin that lays eggs. Reptiles have cold blood in their bodies.

Snakes, lizards, and tortoises are reptiles.

remove (verb)
If you remove something you take it off or take it away.

Dad began to remove the mirror from the wall.

rescue (verb)
To rescue someone is to save that person from danger.

Firefighters rescue people from fires.

repair (verb)
If you repair something you fix it so that it works again.

I have special tools to repair my bike.

reservoir (noun)
A reservoir is a big lake that is built to store water.

The water from your faucets might come from a reservoir.

a b c d e f g h i j k l m n o p q **r** s t u v w x y z

restaurant (noun)

A restaurant is a place where you buy a meal and then eat it.

A restaurant has lots of tables where you sit and eat.

rhinoceros (noun)

A rhinoceros is a large wild animal. It has a horn on the front of its head.

A rhinoceros is often called a rhino for short.

ribbon (noun)

A ribbon is a long, thin piece of material. You use a ribbon to tie something or to decorate it.

The flowers are tied with a red ribbon.

rice (noun)

Rice is a seed from a plant that grows in hot places. You cook and eat rice.

Can you eat rice with two chopsticks?

rich (adjective)

If you are rich you have a lot of money.

The rich king had lots of gold coins.

ride (verb)

To ride is to sit on something as it moves along. You can ride a horse by sitting on its back.

Do you know how to ride a horse?

right (adjective)
Right means correct. If something is right it is not wrong.

A check mark shows that the answer is right.

right
Right is also the opposite to left. Most people write with their right hand.

Sam is waving with his right hand.

ring (noun)
A ring is a thin circle of metal that you wear on a finger. Men and women wear rings.

A ring with a bright stone in it will sparkle.

ring (verb)
If something rings it makes a sound like a bell.

A doorbell rings when you press it.

river (noun)
A river is a large amount of water that flows over the land. Most rivers flow into the ocean.

Fish live in this river.

road (noun)
A road is a long stretch of ground. Vehicles drive along it. The surface of a road is hard.

Be careful when you cross the road!

a b c d e f g h i j k l m n o p q **r** s t u v w x y z

robot (noun)
A robot is a machine that does jobs for us. Robots in factories are controlled by computers.

This robot is painting a new car.

rock (noun)
A rock is a large, heavy stone.

There are big rocks on this seashore.

rocket (noun)
A rocket can fly straight up into space from the ground. Some rockets take people up into space.

A rocket makes a lot of noise when it leaves the ground.

rocking chair (noun)
A rocking chair moves backward and forward. It has curved pieces of wood under its legs.

It is comfortable to sit in a rocking chair.

rocking horse (noun)
A rocking horse is a wooden toy horse. It moves backward and forward when you sit on it.

It's fun to ride on a rocking horse.

roll (verb)
To roll is to turn over and over like a wheel.

A ball will roll along the ground if you push it.

rollerblade (noun)

A rollerblade is a boot with a row of wheels on the bottom. You can go very fast on rollerblades.

You wear knee pads with your rollerblades in case you fall over.

roof (noun)

A roof is the top part of a building. It sits on top of the walls.

Birds like to sit on the roof of a house.

room (noun)

A room is a space inside a house. It has walls, a door, and a floor.

A dolls' house has lots of different rooms.

rope (noun)

Rope is very thick, strong string.

Lots of threads are twisted together to make a rope.

rough (adjective)

Rough means bumpy and not smooth.

The path was rough and full of stones.

round (adjective)

If something is round it is shaped like a circle or a ball.

These party balloons are round.

a b c d e f g h i j k l m n o p q r s t u v w x y z

row (noun)

A row is a straight line of people or things.

These baby ducks are walking in a row.

row (verb)

To row a boat is to move it along by pulling and pushing oars. You usually row with two oars.

Do you know how to row?

rug (noun)

A rug is a small blanket or mat. You can put a rug on a bed or on the ground.

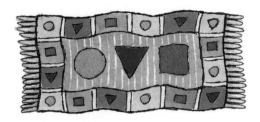

I have a colorful rug on my bedroom floor.

ruler (noun)

In some countries, a ruler is a person who is the head of the country.

Kings and queens are rulers.

A ruler is also a flat piece of wood or plastic with marks on the side. You use a ruler to draw straight lines and to measure things.

Can you draw a straight line without a ruler?

run (verb)

To run is to move very quickly on your legs. It is faster to run than to walk.

A cheetah can run faster than any other animal.

Ss

sack (noun)
A sack is a large bag for holding things. It might be made of paper, material, or plastic.

Santa Claus carries a sack of presents.

saddle (noun)
A saddle is the seat you sit on when you ride a horse or a bicycle.

A saddle helps a cowboy stay on his horse.

sad (adjective)
A sad person is not happy. People do not feel good when they are sad.

Some people cry when they feel sad.

safe (adjective)
If something is safe it means it cannot hurt you and there is no danger.

A seat belt helps to keep a baby safe in the car.

a b c d e f g h i j k l m n o p q r **s** t u v w x y z

safety pin (noun)

A safety pin is a pin that closes at one end. You can use a safety pin to attach things to your clothes.

The badge has a safety pin on the back.

sail (noun)

A sail is a piece of cloth that is joined to a boat. Wind blows into the sail and makes the boat move.

Sails are often bright colors.

sailor (noun)

A sailor is a person who sails a boat.

The sailors on this sailboat are putting up their sails.

salad (noun)

A salad is a dish made mostly of uncooked food. You usually eat salad cold.

You often find lettuce and tomatoes in a salad.

salt (noun)

Salt is a white powder or tiny white grains. You add salt to food to make it taste better.

Maria sprinkles some salt over her food.

sand (noun)

Sand is made of millions of tiny grains of rock. Some deserts and beaches are made of sand.

You can build a sandcastle with sand.

sandal (noun)

A sandal is a shoe with straps. Sandals keep your feet cool in warm weather.

When you wear sandals you can see your toes.

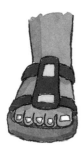 

satellite (noun)

A satellite is an object that moves around a planet in space. It can be man-made or something natural.

A man-made satellite flies high above the Earth.

sandcastle (noun)

A sandcastle is a shape that you make with wet sand. You fill a pail with sand and turn it upside down.

The water may wash away your sandcastle on the beach.

saucepan (noun)

A saucepan is a container for cooking. It has a lid and a handle. You can heat up food in a saucepan.

A saucepan sits on the top of a stove.

sandwich (noun)

A sandwich is two pieces of bread, with a food such as ham or cheese in the middle.

I have a cheese and tomato sandwich for my lunch.

saucer (noun)

A saucer is a small, round dish. A cup can fit on top of a saucer.

A cup of tea might have a saucer with it.

a b c d e f g h i j k l m n o p q r **s** t u v w x y z

a b c d e f g h i j k l m n o p q r s t u v w x y z

saw (noun)
A saw has a handle, a flat metal part, and teeth along one edge. You use it to cut wood and other materials.

You need a big saw to cut through a large piece of wood.

scale (noun)
You use a scale to find out how heavy a person or a thing is.

I weighed the cherries on a scale.

scarecrow (noun)
A scarecrow is a funny, pretend person on a stick. Scarecrows scare away the birds from the farmer's crops.

A scarecrow usually wears old clothes and a silly hat.

scared (verb)
If you are scared you are frightened of someone or something.

Little Miss Muffet was scared of the spider.

scarf (noun)
A scarf is a long piece of cloth that you wear around your neck. It keeps you warm.

Do you wear a scarf when you go out in the snow?

school (noun)
A school is a place where children go to learn. They learn to read, write, and do math.

Do you have lots of friends at your school?

154

scissors (noun)

Scissors have two blades that are joined together. You use scissors to cut paper, hair, and other things.

You can cut paper into pieces with scissors.

screw (noun)

A screw is like a thick nail, but it is not smooth. A screw joins two things together.

A screw is made of metal.

screwdriver (noun)

A screwdriver is a tool for fitting a screw tightly into a hole. You turn a screwdriver round and round to make it work.

You use a screwdriver to tighten a screw.

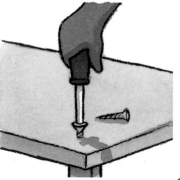

sea (noun)

The sea is all the salty water around the land. It is another word for the ocean. Ships sail on the sea.

Dolphins live in the sea.

seagull (noun)

A seagull is a large bird with gray and white feathers. It has a sharp beak to catch fish.

You can often see seagulls on the shore.

seahorse (noun)

A seahorse is a small fish with a curly tail. Its head is shaped like a horse.

Seahorses are very pretty fish.

a b c d e f g h i j k l m n o p q r s t u v w x y z

a b c d e f g h i j k l m n o p q r **s** t u v w x y z

seal (noun)

A seal is an animal that lives in the ocean and on land. It has flippers to help it swim.

In very cold places seals live on the ice.

seat (noun)

A seat is something you sit on, such as a chair or a stool.

There are lots of empty seats around the table.

seat belt (noun)

A seat belt is a special strap in a car or a bus. It stops you from being hurt if there is an accident.

When you sit in a car, you must always fasten your seat belt.

seaweed (noun)

Seaweed is a plant that grows in the ocean. It never has any flowers.

Seaweed grows on the bottom of the ocean.

see (verb)

To see is to use your eyes to look at something.

Some people need glasses to help them see properly.

seed (noun)

A seed is the part of a plant that can grow into another plant. You can buy seeds in packets.

Carrot seeds are very small.

seesaw (noun)
A seesaw is a wooden or metal plank that two people sit on. Each person sits at one of the ends. When one person goes up, the other person comes down.

Is there a seesaw in a park near you?

shadow (noun)
A shadow is a dark shape that is made behind something when light shines on it.

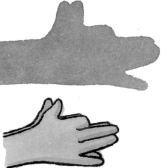

Try making a shadow with your hands on a wall.

sell (verb)
To sell something is to give it to somebody for money.

The baker sells freshly baked bread in his store.

shake (verb)
To shake is to quickly move something backward and forward or from side to side.

Carly shakes the maracas in the school band.

sew (verb)
To sew is to join pieces of cloth together. You use a needle and thread to sew.

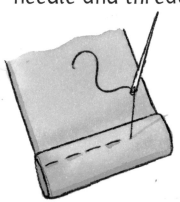

When you sew you make a row of little stitches.

shallow (adjective)
Shallow means not very deep.

The water in a puddle is shallow, not deep.

a b c d e f g h i j k l m n o p q r s t u v w x y z

shampoo (noun)
Shampoo is a liquid soap. You use shampoo to wash your hair.

Shampoo makes bubbles when you rub it.

shape (noun)
A shape is the outline of something. Everything has a shape.

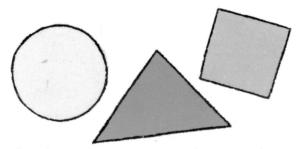

Circles, squares, and triangles are shapes.

share (verb)
To share is to give to others.

Julia shares her birthday cake with her best friend.

shark (noun)
A shark is a big, fierce fish. It has lots of sharp teeth and is not at all friendly.

Some sharks are very dangerous and can kill people.

sharp (adjective)
When something is sharp it is pointed and could prick you.

Be careful of sharp knives!

shed (noun)
A shed is a small, wooden building in a yard or a garden.

A shed is a good place to keep garden tools.

sheep (noun)
A sheep is a farm animal with a woolly coat. We get wool, milk, and meat from sheep.

A baby sheep is called a lamb.

sheet (noun)
A sheet is a large, thin piece of material, such as cotton or plastic.

What color is the sheet on your bed?

shelf (noun)
A shelf is a flat piece of wood or metal. A shelf is attached to a wall or is inside a closet.

Andrew took a book from the top shelf.

shell (noun)
A shell is a thin, hard part on some animals. It fits around the body of an animal such as a crab or a snail.

Shells can be lots of different shapes and colors.

shield (noun)
A shield is a large piece of metal or wood that soldiers used to carry. It protects a soldier's body.

Long ago, a knight in armor carried a shield.

shine (verb)
To shine is to give out light. Lamps shine in the street when it gets dark.

You can shine a flashlight to read in the dark.

a b c d e f g h i j k l m n o p q r **s** t u v w x y z

ship (noun)
A ship is a large boat that can only sail in deep water.

This pirate ship is flying a pirate flag.

shipwreck (noun)
A shipwreck is a ship that has fallen to the bottom of the ocean.

Fish often swim in and out of a shipwreck.

shirt (noun)
You wear a shirt on the top part of your body. Some shirts have buttons down the front.

People like to wear colorful shirts in the summer.

shiver (verb)
To shiver is to shake all over. You cannot keep still when you shiver.

You will shiver if you are very cold.

shoe (noun)
A shoe keeps your foot warm and dry. Shoes come in lots of different colors and shapes.

How many pairs of shoes do you have?

shoelace (noun)
A shoelace is a kind of string that you use to tie up a shoe.

My sneakers have thick, white shoelaces.

a b c d e f g h i j k l m n o p q r s t u v w x y z

shoot (noun)
A shoot is a small plant that is just starting to grow.

A panda likes to eat bamboo shoots.

shoulder (noun)
Your shoulder is the place where your arm joins the rest of your body. You have two shoulders.

Dad carried the heavy sack on his shoulder.

shop (noun)
A shop is a building where you can buy things. There are lots of shops in a big city.

A pet shop sells animals and petfood.

shout (verb)
To shout is to call out very loudly. People often shout when they are angry.

Do you shout to your friends at recess?

shorts (noun)
Shorts are pants with legs that only come down to your knees.

People wear shorts when the weather is hot.

shovel (noun)
A shovel is a tool with a long handle and a flat blade. You use a shovel to dig and to move soil.

You can use a shovel to clear away the snow.

a b c d e f g h i j k l m n o p q r s t u v w x y z

show (verb)

To show something is to let another person see it.

Do you show your paintings to your mom or dad?

shower (noun)

A shower sprays hot or cold water all over you. You stand under a shower to wash yourself.

The water comes out of tiny holes in the shower.

shut (adjective)

When something is shut it is not open. You cannot walk through a shut door.

Make sure the door is shut when you leave the house!

sign (noun)

A sign is a notice that tells you something. A sign gives you a street name or the name of a store.

A sign by the road helps drivers find their way.

signal (noun)

A signal is a message that tells you something. A flashing light on the back of a car is a signal.

The flashing signal says that the car is turning left.

signpost (noun)

A signpost is a sign that shows the way to somewhere.

You might see a signpost like this at the zoo.

sing (verb)
To sing is to make music with your voice. Birds like to sing.

Lots of people sing together in a choir.

sit (verb)
To sit is to rest your bottom on something. You sit on a chair.

Our cat likes to sit on my lap.

sink (noun)
The sink is the place in your kitchen where you wash the dishes. You fill a sink with water from the faucet.

Do you put your dirty dishes in the sink?

skate (verb)
To skate means to move around on ice. You need to wear special boots to skate.

Can you skate as well as these two skaters?

sink (verb)
To sink is to move downward. If you throw a pebble into water it will sink under the water.

A hook on a fishing line sinks in the water.

skateboard (noun)
A skateboard is a flat plank with wheels at each end. You stand on a skateboard and ride along on it.

You can learn to do clever tricks on a skateboard.

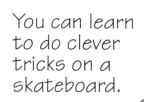

a b c d e f g h i j k l m n o p q r **s** t u v w x y z

skeleton (noun)

A skeleton is all the bones in your body joined together. People and lots of animals have a skeleton.

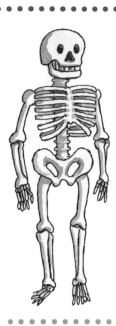

You have over 200 bones in your skeleton.

ski (noun)

A ski is a long piece of wood, metal, or plastic. You use skis to move over snow or water.

You attach snow skis onto special boots.

skip (verb)

To skip is to jump lightly from one foot to the other. You can skip with a jump rope.

Some children skip rope very fast.

skirt (noun)

A skirt is a piece of clothing that fits around the waist and hangs down.

Natalie wears a short, polka dot skirt.

skull (noun)

Your skull is a set of hard bones around your head. It protects your brain.

A pirate flag has a picture of a skull on it.

skunk (noun)

A skunk is a small black and white animal with a bushy tail.

A skunk sprays a very smelly liquid when it is scared.

sky (noun)
Sky is the space you see above you when you are outside. At night the sky is full of stars.

At night the sky looks very dark.

sleep (verb)
You sleep when you are tired. When you sleep your eyes close and your body is still.

Our dog likes to sleep in his basket.

skyscraper (noun)
A skyscraper is a very tall building. Most skyscrapers are built in the middle of big cities.

Some skyscrapers are so tall that they seem to reach the clouds.

sleeping bag (noun)
A sleeping bag is a big bag made from warm cloth. It is open at one end so that you can fit inside it.

If you go camping you might sleep in a sleeping bag.

sled (noun)
A sled is a piece of wood or plastic that can slide over snow and ice. You can sit on a sled.

It is fun to play on a sled in the snow.

sleeve (noun)
A sleeve is the part of a coat or shirt that covers your arm.

A sleeve can be long or short.

a b c d e f g h i j k l m n o p q r s t u v w x y z

slice (noun)
A slice is a thin piece of something. A slice is cut from a bigger piece.

You can cut a slice off a loaf of bread.

slide (noun)
A slide has a tall ladder and a long, smooth ramp. You climb up the ladder and go down the long, shiny slide.

I like the big slide in the park.

sling (noun)
A sling is a piece of cloth stretched around an arm and a shoulder. If you break your arm you need to wear a sling.

A sling keeps a broken arm safe until it is better.

slipper (noun)
A slipper is a soft shoe that you wear indoors.

Are your slippers cozy and soft like these ones?

slow (adjective)
Slow means not fast. A slow person does not move fast.

A tortoise is a very slow animal.

slug (noun)
A slug is an animal that looks like a snail with no shell. Slugs like to eat plants.

A slug likes to eat leaves in the yard.

small (adjective)

Small means not big. Small is the same as little.

I am small, but my mom and dad are big.

smell (verb)

You smell with your nose. You might like to smell a flower or some scent.

Mia likes to smell pretty flowers.

smile (verb)

When you smile the corners of your mouth go up. You smile when you are happy.

People smile when someone takes their picture.

smoke (noun)

Smoke is a dark cloud that comes from a fire. Something gives off smoke when it is burning.

Smoke from a bonfire goes up into the air.

smooth (adjective)

Something is smooth if it has no bumps or lumps in it.

It is easier to skate on smooth ice.

snack (noun)

A snack is a small amount of food that you might eat between meals.

An apple makes a good snack.

abcdefghijklmnopqr**s**tuvwxyz

snail (noun)
A snail is a small animal with a shell on its back. A snail moves very slowly.

Snails like to eat juicy, young plants.

snake (noun)
A snake is an animal with a long, thin body. It has no legs. A snake slides along the ground.

A snake can wind its body around the branch of a tree.

sneeze (verb)
When you sneeze, air suddenly comes out of your mouth and nose. It sounds as if you are saying "A-choo!"

You might sneeze if dust goes up your nose.

sniff (verb)
To sniff is to breathe in quickly through your nose. You might sniff a strong smell.

A dog sniffs to find the smell of its bone.

snorkel (noun)
A snorkel is a tube that helps you to breathe underwater.

You use a snorkel and a mask underwater.

snow (noun)
Snow is soft, white flakes that fall from the sky. It is frozen rain. Snow comes when the weather is very cold.

Snow is good for making snowballs.

snowman (noun)

A snowman is a shape made of snow. When there is lots of snow you can push it together to build a snowman.

A snowman often wears a hat and a scarf, and has a carrot for his nose.

soap (noun)

You use soap to wash and to make things clean. You mix it with water. Soap often smells sweet.

You make bubbles when you wash with soap and water.

soccer (noun)

Soccer is a game that two teams play on a grassy field. Each team tries to kick the ball into the other team's goal.

You wear special boots when you play soccer.

sock (noun)

You wear a sock on your foot. It is made of soft cloth. You put on your socks before you put on your shoes.

Some socks have bright colors and patterns on them.

sofa (noun)

A sofa is a big, comfortable seat. Two or three people can sit on a sofa.

A sofa might have cushions on it.

soft (adjective)

Soft is something that is not hard. A pillow is soft.

My teddy bear is soft and cuddly.

a b c d e f g h i j k l m n o p q r **s** t u v w x y z

soil (noun)
Soil is another word for the earth in the ground. Plants grow in soil.

A gardener digs the soil with a shovel.

somersault (verb)
When you somersault you roll over forward or backward. To somersault you turn head over heels.

A gymnast tries to somersault high in the air.

soldier (noun)
A soldier is a person who is in an army. Soldiers train to fight battles.

A soldier learns to march in a line.

sore (adjective)
When something is sore it hurts.

Your knee feels sore if you fall over and cut it.

sole (noun)
Your sole is the bottom of your foot. It is the part that touches the ground.

Is the sole of your foot ticklish?

soup (noun)
Soup is a tasty liquid made of food. You can use vegetables or meat to make soup.

You eat soup from a bowl.

sour (adjective)
If something is sour it does not taste sweet. A sour food has a bitter taste.

A lemon tastes sour.

sow (noun)
A sow is a female pig.

A sow might have lots of baby pigs.

sow (verb)
To sow is to put seeds into the ground. You sow seeds so that they will grow into plants.

If you sow a seed and water it, it will slowly grow.

space (noun)
Space is the huge area far above the Earth. The Moon and the stars are in space.

Some people have walked in space.

A space is also an empty area. You look for a space when you go to a parking lot.

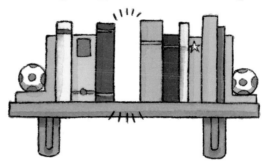

There is a space on my shelf for one more book.

spaceship (noun)
A spaceship is a vehicle that takes people into space.

A spaceship has big engines to lift it off the ground.

a b c d e f g h i j k l m n o p q r **s** t u v w x y z

spaghetti (noun)
Spaghetti is a food that looks like long pieces of string. It is hard before you cook it, but it goes soft when cooked.

It is not easy to eat spaghetti.

speak (verb)
To speak is to say words. You use your mouth to speak.

You have to speak into a telephone.

spark (noun)
A spark is a tiny, hot speck. Sparks shoot out of something that burns.

Lots of sparks shoot out of a sparkler.

speed (verb)
To speed is to travel very fast. A person who speeds on the road is driving too fast.

The driver speeds around the race track.

sparrow (noun)
A sparrow is a small, brown bird. You might see sparrows in the park.

A sparrow might hop close to you.

spell (verb)
When you spell a word you say or write each letter. You spell the letters in the right order.

Can you spell the word "kneel?"

spend (verb)
To spend is to give money to buy something you want.

If you go shopping you will spend money.

spoon (noun)
A spoon has a long handle and a round part at one end. You use a spoon to eat foods such as soup, ice cream, and cereal.

Spoons are made of metal, plastic, or wood.

spider (noun)
A spider is a small animal with eight legs. A spider makes a web to catch flies to eat.

Some people are scared of spiders. Are you?

spot (noun)
A spot is a small, round mark. Some cloths and papers have a pattern of spots on them.

My favorite sweater has purple spots.

spill (verb)
If you spill something, you let it fall out of its container

The juice spills out of the carton.

squirrel (noun)
A squirrel is a small, furry animal with a long, fat tail. It loves to eat nuts.

Most squirrels are gray but some are red.

a b c d e f g h i j k l m n o p q r s t u v w x y z

stable (noun)
A stable is a building where a horse lives.

The horse looked out of his stable.

stamp (noun)
A stamp is a small piece of colored paper. You stick a stamp on a letter or package before you mail it.

You have to put a lot of stamps on a big, heavy package.

stadium (noun)
A stadium is a large building where you can see sports events. It usually has a big field with lots of seats around it.

Big crowds of people can sit inside a stadium.

stand (verb)
To stand is to be on your feet. If you stand you are not sitting down.

Michael stands and waits for the bus each day.

stair (noun)
A stair is a step that you walk up. You have to climb the stairs to get to rooms at the top of a house.

At bedtime I climb each stair very slowly.

star (noun)
A star is a small, bright light in the sky. You can see stars at night when it is dark.

There are too many stars in the sky to count them.

starfish (noun)

A starfish is an animal that lives in the ocean. It has five arms and looks like a star.

A starfish does not look like a fish at all.

station (noun)

A station is a place where trains and buses pick up passengers. You can buy your tickets at a station.

If you want to catch a train you should go to a station.

statue (noun)

A statue is a model of a person or an animal. Most statues are made from stone, metal, or wood.

You might see a statue of a famous person in a city.

steam (noun)

Steam is a hot, white cloud of gas. It comes from boiling water.

Steam comes out when water boils in a pan.

steering wheel (noun)

A steering wheel is the wheel in the inside of a vehicle. You turn the steering wheel to make the vehicle go where you want.

The tractor has a big, red steering wheel.

stem (noun)

A stem is the long, thin part of a plant that grows up from the ground. Leaves and flowers grow on a stem.

You hold the stem when you pick a flower.

a b c d e f g h i j k l m n o p q r s t u v w x y z

stencil (noun)

A stencil is a piece of paper or plastic with a picture cut out of it. You use a stencil to draw a picture onto paper.

Tom uses a stencil to draw a picture of a boat.

stew (noun)

A stew is hot food made of meat and vegetables. You cook the food in a stew for a long time.

You cook stew in a big pot.

stick (noun)

A stick is a long, thin piece of wood. You might find a stick under a tree.

If you throw a stick our dog will bring it back.

stir (verb)

To stir is to move things around so that they mix together.

A cook stirs the food in the pan.

stone (noun)

A stone is a small piece of rock. Stones are many different sizes and shapes.

There are lots of stones in the ground.

stool (noun)

A stool is a small seat with no back or arms.

Some stools have only three legs.

storm (noun)

A storm is very bad weather, with lots of rain and strong winds.

There may be thunder and lightning in a storm.

story (noun)

A story tells you about things that have happened. Stories are not always true. You can read a story in a book.

The children listen to a story at the end of the day.

straight (adjective)

A straight line has no bends in it. You use a ruler to draw a straight line.

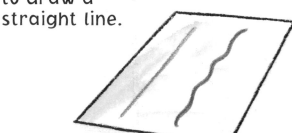

The blue line is straight but the red one is squiggly.

strawberry (noun)

A strawberry is a juicy, red fruit. It is sweet to eat. You do not have to cook strawberries.

Strawberries grow on the ground, so they are easy to pick.

street (noun)

A street is a road in a city or town. A street often has buildings on each side.

There are lots of stores in this street.

stretcher (noun)

A stretcher is a thin bed that you can lift up and carry along. You carry sick people on a stretcher.

The two men carried the stretcher to an ambulance.

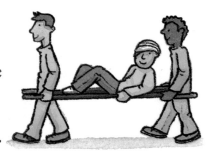

a b c d e f g h i j k l m n o p q r **s** t u v w x y z

string (noun)
String is a long, thin rope that you use to tie things together.

The balloons are tied up with string.

stripe (noun)
A stripe is a thin line of color.

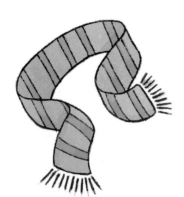

This scarf has green stripes on it.

strong (adjective)
If you are strong you can carry heavy things. A strong person can do lots of hard work.

A farmer has to be very strong.

submarine (noun)
A submarine is a boat that can move under the ocean. It can travel along the top of the ocean as well.

A submarine can dive down very deep.

sugar (noun)
Sugar is a sweet powder that you can mix with other foods. You use sugar to make foods and drinks taste sweeter.

My mom puts a spoonful of sugar in her tea.

suit (noun)
A suit is a set of clothes that match. A suit has a jacket and pants or a skirt.

My dad wears a suit when he goes to work.

suitcase (noun)

A suitcase is a big bag with a handle on it. It opens up so that you can put clothes inside.

Do you take a big suitcase when you go on vacation?

sum (noun)

A sum is the answer you get when you add together numbers.

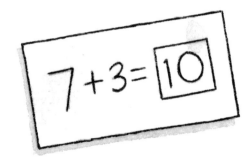

The sum of 7 and 3 is 10.

sun (noun)

The sun shines in the sky in the day. It keeps us warm and gives us light.

The sun is like a bright yellow ball in the sky.

sundial (noun)

A sundial is a type of outdoor clock. As the sun moves across the sky, a shadow on the sundial shows what time it is.

A sundial only works when the sun is shining.

sunflower (noun)

A sunflower is a tall plant with big, yellow flowers.

A sunflower can grow to be 10 feet high.

sunglasses (noun)

You wear sunglasses to protect your eyes from bright sunshine. When you wear sunglasses everything looks darker.

You should wear sunglasses on a sunny day.

sunset (noun)

Sunset is the time at the end of a day when the sun goes down. At sunset it starts to grow dark.

The sky might be orange and pink at the sunset.

supermarket (noun)

A supermarket is a large store that sells foods and many things for the home.

We put our shopping in a cart at the supermarket.

surf (verb)

When you surf you travel along a wave in the sea. You stand or sit on a special board to surf.

Would you like to surf like this?

surprise (noun)

A surprise is something that you do not expect to happen.

Dad says he has a big surprise for me.

swan (noun)

A swan is a large bird with a long neck. It lives in rivers and lakes. Swans have big, strong wings.

There are swans on the river near my home.

sweep (verb)

You use a broom to sweep a floor. When you sweep you make something clean and neat.

Dylan sweeps the leaves when they fall off the trees.

sweet (adjective)

Something that is sweet has a taste of sugar. Sweet is the opposite of sour.

My dad likes to drink sweet tea.

swim (verb)

When you swim you use your arms and legs to move through water.

I like to swim in the ocean.

swimming pool (noun)

A swimming pool is a place where you go to swim. The water at one end of a swimming pool is usually deep.

We like to sit on the side of the swimming pool.

swing (noun)

A swing has two thick pieces of rope or metal, and a piece of wood for the seat. You sit on a swing and move back and forth.

If you go high on a swing, remember to hold on tightly.

switch (noun)

You use a switch to turn things on and off. You press a switch to turn on a radio or a light.

The light comes on when you press the switch.

sword (noun)

A sword is a long, thin piece of metal. It has a sharp point at one end and a handle at the other. Long ago, soldiers used to fight with swords.

The handle of this sword is made of gold.

a b c d e f g h i j k l m n o p q r **s** t u v w x y z

abcdefghijklmnopqrstuvwxyz

table (noun)
A table has a flat top and usually four legs. You sit at a table to eat your meals.

What can you see on top of this table?

tail (noun)
A tail is the long, thin part at the back of some animals. A mouse has a long tail. A pig has a curly tail.

A dog wags its tail when it is happy.

tadpole (noun)
A tadpole is a baby frog. It lives in water and has no legs at first.

When a tadpole grows legs and loses its tail, it turns into a frog.

tailor (noun)
A tailor is a person who uses a sewing machine to make clothes.

The tailor sews the sleeve of a new suit.

talk (verb)
To talk is to say words. When you talk you speak words to another person.

My sister likes to talk on the phone.

tanker (noun)
A tanker is a large ship or a large truck. It carries liquids such as oil or milk.

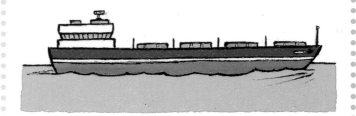

This tanker carries oil across the ocean.

tall (adjective)
Tall is very high. A tall person is not short.

There is a tall tower in the middle of the city.

tap (verb)
When you tap something you hit it gently.

Dad taps on the kitchen window.

tambourine (noun)
A tambourine is a round musical instrument. It has metal circles around the edge.

You tap or shake a tambourine to make a noise.

tape measure (noun)
A tape measure is a very long, thin piece of cloth or metal. You use it to measure things.

A tape measure has marks along it to show feet and inches.

target (noun)
A target is something that you try to hit. In archery you shoot at a target.

A black cross marks the middle of the target.

taxi (noun)
A taxi is a car with a driver. The driver takes you where you want to go and then you pay the driver.

A taxi often has a sign on its roof.

tassel (noun)
A tassel is a bunch of threads that are tied at one end. You use tassels to decorate hats and cushions.

My new hat has bright pink tassels.

tea (noun)
Tea is a drink that you make from the leaves of the tea plant and boiling water. The leaves can be inside a small bag.

I drink a mug of tea at breakfast.

taste (verb)
You taste food to see if you like it. You taste with your tongue.

Dad wants to taste the soup before he eats it.

teach (verb)
To teach is to tell or show someone how to do something.

My class teacher teaches me how to read.

184

tear (noun)
A tear is a drop of water that comes from your eye.

Tears run down my cheek when I cry.

teenager (noun)
A teenager is a young person who is between 13 and 19 years old.

Teenagers like to go out with their friends.

tear (verb)
To tear is to pull something apart. If you tear something in half you will have two pieces.

Kate tears her painting because she doesn't like it.

telephone (noun)
A telephone is a machine that lets you talk to people who are in another place.

When a telephone rings, you pick it up.

teddy bear (noun)
A teddy bear is a furry toy. Teddy bears can be small or large, and they are all cuddly.

My teddy bear sleeps in my bed at night.

telescope (noun)
A telescope lets you see things a long way away. It has a long, thin tube that you look through.

The stars look bigger when you see them through a telescope.

a b c d e f g h i j k l m n o p q r s **t** u v w x y z

television (noun)
A television is a machine that brings you pictures and sounds from other places.

Which shows do you like on television?

tell (verb)
To tell is to speak a story or to give some news to another person.

My grandpa tells me stories at bedtime.

tennis (noun)
Tennis is a ball game. You play it on a court with a net across the middle. Each player has a racket to hit the ball.

Two or four people can play a game of tennis.

tent (noun)
A tent is a little house made of soft cloth. You can fold up a tent and carry it.

You can sleep outside in a tent.

test (noun)
A test is a group of questions or problems. A test is a way of finding out what someone knows.

I wrote down the answers to the test.

theater (noun)
A theater is a place where you watch a show or a play. Inside a theater there is a stage and lots of seats.

They danced on a big stage inside the theater.

thermometer (noun)

A thermometer tells you how hot or cold something is. A nurse or doctor may put it in your mouth if you are sick.

A thermometer tells you if a sick person is running a fever.

thigh (noun)

Your thigh is the top part of your leg. It is between your knee and your hip.

Your thigh is above your knee.

thick (adjective)

If something is thick it is wide. Thick is the opposite of thin. Your arm is thick but your finger is thin.

A thick book has a lot of pages.

thin (adjective)

Thin means not fat. A pencil is thin.

The monster has long, thin arms and legs.

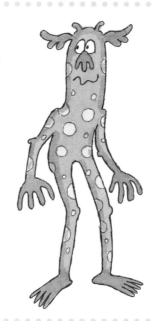

thief (noun)

A thief is a person who takes things that belong to another person. A thief steals things.

A thief took my new bicycle.

thirsty (adjective)

If you are thirsty you want a drink. People are often thirsty in hot weather.

After a long walk I feel thirsty.

thistle (noun)

A thistle is a plant with prickly leaves. It has a purple, white, blue, or yellow flower on the top.

Thistles grow in wild places.

thorn (noun)

A thorn is a sharp point that grows on some plants.

Be careful you do not prick your finger on a rose thorn!

thread (noun)

A thread is a long, thin piece of cloth. A thread can be made of cotton, silk, wool, or nylon.

I did some sewing with the blue thread.

throne (noun)

A throne is a special chair for a king or a queen. A throne is used for an important event.

The golden throne has purple cushions.

throw (verb)

When you throw you send something from your hand. You make it go a long way in the air.

My sister likes me to throw the ball to her.

thumb (noun)

A thumb is the thick, short finger on your hand. You have two thumbs.

My big brother sticks up his thumb when he wants to say "Yes!"

thumbtack (noun)

A thumbtack is a small pin with a flat, round top. You use a thumbtack to pin a picture onto a bulletin board.

A thumbtack has a sharp point at one end.

thunder (noun)

Thunder is a very loud, banging noise in the sky. You hear thunder when there is a storm.

The loud thunder woke me up.

ticket (noun)

A ticket is a small piece of paper that shows you have paid to do something. You buy a ticket when you travel on a bus or a train.

I am buying a ticket for the movie.

tide (noun)

The tide is the change of the ocean when it moves up and down the beach.

When the tide goes out you can walk across the sand.

tie (noun)

A tie is a long, thin piece of cloth. You wear a tie around the collar of a shirt.

Jack's tie has red and yellow stripes.

tie (verb)

If you tie something you make a knot or a bow in it. You can tie a ribbon around a gift.

The sailor ties a knot in the rope.

a b c d e f g h i j k l m n o p q r s **t** u v w x y z

tiger (noun)
A tiger is a large wild animal. It is like a big cat with an orange coat and black stripes.

A tiger is a strong and fierce animal.

tight (adjective)
If something is tight it fits very closely. If your shoes are tight they may be too small for you.

My coat is so tight that I can't close it up.

tile (noun)
A tile is a small piece of material. It can be hard or soft. You use tiles to cover floors and walls.

The roof of our house is made of red tiles.

tiptoe (verb)
To tiptoe is to walk very quietly on your toes.

I have to tiptoe past the baby when she's asleep.

toad (noun)
A toad is like a big frog. A toad crawls about on land, but a frog jumps.

If you touch a toad you can feel the bumps under its skin.

toadstool (noun)
A toadstool is a kind of mushroom. Most toadstools are poisonous so you must never eat them.

We found a bright red toadstool in the woods.

toast (noun)
Toast is a cooked slice of bread. When you make toast the bread becomes crisp and brown.

The toast popped out of the toaster.

tomato (noun)
A tomato is a soft, round fruit. Tomatoes are red, and they grow on vines.

You can cut up a tomato and eat it in a salad.

toddler (noun)
A toddler is a young child who has just learned how to walk.

A toddler can walk without help from a grown-up.

tongue (noun)
Your tongue is the soft, pink part inside your mouth. Your tongue helps you taste your food.

It is rude to stick out your tongue!

toe (noun)
You have five toes on the end of each foot. Your toes are all different sizes.

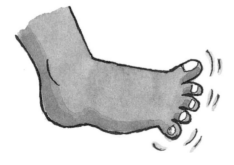

Can you wiggle your toes?

tool (noun)
A tool is something that helps you do a job. Hammers, saws, and screwdrivers are tools.

My dad keeps his tools in a toolbox.

tooth (noun)

A tooth is one of the hard, white parts in your mouth. The plural of tooth is teeth. You use your teeth to chew your food.

You should brush your teeth twice each day.

toothbrush (noun)

A toothbrush has a small brush at one end and a handle. You use it to brush your teeth.

You put toothpaste on the end of your toothbrush.

top (noun)

The top is the highest part of a thing. If you walk to the top of the hill you get to the highest point.

She put the box on the top of the closet.

tornado (noun)

A tornado is a very strong wind. It blows round and round in circles. A tornado can blow over trees and houses.

A tornado blows out of a big, dark cloud.

tortoise (noun)

A tortoise is an animal with a hard, thick shell on its back. A tortoise tucks its head into the shell when it sleeps.

A tortoise walks very slowly.

toucan (noun)

A toucan is a brightly colored bird. It has a very large beak. Toucans live in hot jungles.

A toucan can crack a nut in its beak.

towel (noun)
A towel is a cloth that you use to dry yourself. Towels are soft and colorful.

Do you have a favorite towel in your home?

tower (noun)
A tower is a tall, thin building. You can see a tower from a long way away because it is so high.

Rapunzel lived in the top of a tower.

toy (noun)
A toy is a thing that a child plays with. Dolls, blocks, train sets, and jack-in-the-boxes are toys.

You often keep toys in a toybox.

tractor (noun)
A tractor is a farm machine with big wheels at the back. It pulls heavy loads and other machines.

The farmer drives his tractor across the field.

traffic (noun)
Traffic is all the moving cars, buses, trucks, and motorcycles that go along the roads.

There is a lot of traffic in the center of the city.

trailer (noun)
A trailer is a vehicle that a car can pull along. It is a kind of home. Some people spend their vacation inside a trailer.

We stay in our trailer each summer.

train (noun)

A train moves along a railway track. It has an engine that pulls train cars. People ride in a train from place to place.

A train goes fast so you get to places quickly.

trampoline (noun)

When you go on a trampoline you jump up and down on it. A trampoline is made of strong material inside a frame.

I love to jump on my trampoline.

travel (verb)

To travel is to go from one place to another.

I travel with my big sister when I go on vacation.

trawler (noun)

A trawler is a fishing boat. It pulls a big net through the ocean to catch fish.

The hungry seagulls fly over the trawler.

tray (noun)

A tray is a flat piece of wood or plastic. You carry food and drinks on a tray.

There are three milk shakes on the tray.

treasure (noun)

Treasure is gold, money, jewels, and other expensive things. People sometimes hide or bury treasure.

The pirate's chest is full of treasure.

tree (noun)

A tree is a tall plant. It has a thick middle part that is made of wood. Many trees have green leaves.

You can pick red apples from this tree.

trip (noun)

A trip is a short journey to visit a place.

Dad took us on a trip to the zoo.

trick (noun)

A trick is when someone does something clever to entertain people. A magician does magic tricks.

My brother does a funny trick with cards.

trough (noun)

A trough is a long container that holds food or drink for animals. It can be made of stone, wood, or metal.

The farmer pours the food into the trough.

tricycle (noun)

A tricycle is something you ride on. It has one wheel in front and two wheels in back.

How far can you ride your tricycle?

trowel (noun)

A trowel is a small garden tool. It has a curved blade and a short handle.

You use a trowel to dig holes in the soil.

truck (noun)

A truck is a very big vehicle that is open at the back. A truck can carry heavy loads along roads.

The truck was full of big rocks.

true (adjective)

If something is true it is real. A true story is not made up.

Dad read out a true story about a talking parrot.

trumpet (noun)

A trumpet is a musical instrument. It is made of metal. You blow into one end and sounds come out of the other end.

You have to blow hard to play the trumpet.

trunk (noun)

A trunk is the long nose on an elephant. Elephants use their trunks to pick up food and water.

Elephants can spray water out of their trunks.

A trunk is also the thick, straight part of a tree. All the branches of the tree grow out from the trunk.

I tried to put my arms around the tree trunk.

T-shirt (noun)

A T-shirt is a shirt with short sleeves and no collar. T-shirts are often made of cotton.

A T-shirt has no buttons so it's easy to put on.

tube (noun)
A tube is a long container with a cap at one end. It is made of soft plastic or metal.

You squeeze a tube to get the toothpaste out of it.

turn (verb)
When you turn something you move it around. You turn something so it faces another way.

Robert turns his head to look behind.

turtle (noun)
A turtle is an animal with a hard shell on its back. It can live on land or in water.

A mother turtle often lays her eggs in the sand.

tusk (noun)
A tusk is the long, pointed tooth of an elephant or a walrus. It sticks out of the animal's mouth.

An elephant has two hard tusks.

twin (noun)
If you are a twin, you have a brother or sister who was born on the same day as you. Twins have the same mother.

I can't tell which twin is Molly and which one is Mandy.

twist (verb)
To twist is to turn something around and around.

You twist the top of a jar to open it.

a b c d e f g h i j k l m n o p q r s t u v w x y z

ugly (adjective)
Ugly is not pretty or beautiful to look at.

The ugly witch had black teeth and a big nose.

umpire (noun)
An umpire is a person in charge of a game, such as baseball or tennis. The umpire makes sure the players follow the rules.

The umpire sometimes blows a whistle during the game.

umbrella (noun)
An umbrella stops you from getting wet when it rains. You hold an umbrella over your head.

Some umbrellas have pictures on them.

underwear (noun)
Your underwear is the clothes that you wear next to your skin. Your underwear is under your clothes.

Chloe has some pretty pink underwear.

undress (verb)

To undress is to take off your clothes.

You undress when you go to bed.

unicorn (noun)

A unicorn is not a real animal. It looks like a horse with a horn on its head.

You read about unicorns in fairy tales.

uniform (noun)

A uniform is the set of special clothes that you wear when you belong to a group of people.

Police officers, soldiers, and nurses wear a uniform.

untidy (adjective)

Untidy means messy or not neat.

Our toy closet is very untidy.

upset (adjective)

If you are upset you are not happy. You feel sad when you are upset.

I was upset when our dog ran away.

use (verb)

When you use something you do a job with it. You use scissors to cut paper.

I use a toothbrush to brush my teeth.

vacuum cleaner (noun)

A vacuum cleaner sucks up dirt from floors and carpets. It saves you a lot of hard work.

You can clean up quickly if you use a vacuum cleaner.

van (noun)

A van is a car with no seats in the back. People use vans to move things from place to place.

The builder keeps his tools in a blue van.

valley (noun)

A valley is the low land between hills or mountains.

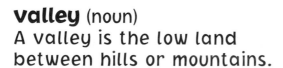

A river often runs through a valley.

vase (noun)

A vase is a container for flowers. You fill a vase with water and put the flowers in it.

When you pick flowers from the yard you put them in a vase.

vegetable (noun)

A vegetable is a part of a plant that you can eat. Potatoes and carrots are vegetables.

Which vegetables do you like to eat?

vehicle (noun)

A vehicle is any machine that carries people or things from place to place on land.

Cars, trains, buses, and trucks are vehicles.

vet (noun)

A vet is a special doctor who looks after animals. You take your pets to a vet when they are sick.

Our cat does not like going to see the vet.

violin (noun)

A violin is a musical instrument with four strings. You play it with a long stick called a bow.

You hold a violin under your chin to play it.

visit (verb)

To visit is to go and see a person or a place.

Dad and I like to visit the art gallery.

voice (noun)

Your voice is the sound you make when you talk or sing.

My brother sings in a loud voice when he is happy.

a b c d e f g h i j k l m n o p q r s t u v w x y z

wait (verb)
To wait is to stay in one place until something happens.

We had to wait for the train to arrive.

waiter (noun)
A waiter is a man who brings food and drinks to you in a restaurant.

The waiter asks us what we want to eat and drink.

waitress (noun)
A waitress is a woman who brings food and drinks to you in a restaurant.

The waitress brings us strawberry milkshakes.

walk (noun)
To walk is to move along by putting one foot in front of the other.

We like to walk in the woods with our dog.

wall (noun)
A wall is made from bricks or stones. You can build a wall around a yard, or between the rooms of a house.

There is a brick wall around our yard.

walrus (noun)
A walrus is a big sea animal that lives in cold places. It has long tusks and flippers instead of feet.

A walrus moves very slowly across the ice.

wand (noun)
A wand is a thin stick. Magicians and fairies have wands.

A magician's wand is black and white.

want (verb)
If you want something you feel that you would like it.

I want some more ice cream.

warm (adjective)
If you feel warm you are not too hot. To be warm is better than to be cold.

When the sun shines you feel warm.

warn (verb)
If you warn someone you tell that person about a danger or a problem.

The red sign warns people that the door is not safe.

a b c d e f g h i j k l m n o p q r s t u v w x y z

wash (verb)

You wash something to make it clean. You wash your hands with soap and water to make them clean.

Do you help wash the car when it's dirty?

washing machine (noun)

A washing machine washes your dirty clothes for you.

A washing machine uses electricity to work.

wasp (noun)

A wasp is a flying insect with black and yellow stripes. A wasp can sting you.

I saw a wasp on a rotten apple.

watch (noun)

A watch is a small clock that you wear on your wrist.

My new watch is blue and yellow.

watch (verb)

To watch is to look at something.

I watch the birds eating food in our yard.

water (noun)

Water is the clear liquid in rivers and oceans. Water falls out of the sky as rain.

Water from the faucet has no taste, but water from the ocean tastes salty.

waterfall (noun)

A waterfall is a place where water falls from a high place to a low place. A waterfall splashes when the water hits the ground.

It is a long way to the bottom of the waterfall.

wear (verb)

When you wear something you are dressed in it.

In the winter I wear my big, red coat.

wave (noun)

A wave is a moving line of water. When the wind blows across the ocean it makes waves.

The sailboat sailed through the big waves.

weather (noun)

The weather is what it is like when you go outside. Rain, snow, and sun are different kinds of weather.

I don't like rainy weather because I have to stay inside.

wave (verb)

To wave is to move your hand from side to side when you say goodbye.

Dad waves to us when he goes to work.

week (noun)

Every week has seven days in it. Sunday is the first day of the week.

Do you know the names of the days of the week?

weigh (verb)

If you weigh something you find out how heavy it is. You use scales to weigh people and things.

I often weigh myself in the bathroom.

well (adjective)

If you are well you look healthy. A person who feels well is not sick.

If you eat lots of fruit it will help you to be well.

wet (adjective)

When something is wet it is covered with water. Wet is not dry.

You get wet in the rain if you forget your umbrella.

whale (noun)

A whale is a huge sea animal. A whale breathes through a hole on the top of its head.

The blue whale is the biggest animal in the world.

wheel (noun)

A wheel is round and it turns. Wheels help cars, bicycles, and tractors move along.

A tractor has big wheels, but a stroller has small ones.

wheelbarrow (noun)

A wheelbarrow is a small cart with one wheel at the front. You use a wheelbarrow to move things in the yard.

A wheelbarrow has two handles so you can push it around.

whisker (noun)

A whisker is a long hair on an animal's face. Whiskers grow near the animal's mouth.

My cat has very long whiskers.

whistle (noun)

You put a whistle in your mouth and blow it. It makes a loud sound.

The teacher blows his whistle at the end of the game.

wild (adjective)

An animal or a plant that is wild is not looked after by people. Wild animals are not pets.

Zebras and giraffes are wild animals.

wind (noun)

Wind is air that moves fast. A strong wind blows things around.

The wind helps dry the wet clothes.

windmill (noun)

A windmill is a tall building with four big sails. The wind turns the sails of a windmill to work the machines inside it.

Have you ever seen a windmill working?

window (noun)

A window is an opening in a wall. A window usually has glass in it to let in the light.

It is a good idea to open a window on a warm day.

wing (noun)

A wing is the part on the body of a bird or an insect that lets it fly. Birds have two wings but butterflies have four.

A bird flaps its wings when it wants to fly.

A wing is also a long, flat part on the side of an airplane. An airplane has two wings to make it fly.

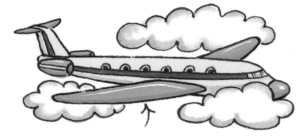

The airplane has bright green wings.

witch (noun)

A witch is a make-believe person in a story. Witches wear tall, pointed hats and fly on broomsticks.

A witch often has a black cat with her.

wizard (noun)

A wizard is a make-believe person who does magic. You read about wizards in stories.

A wizard can do clever, magic tricks.

woman (noun)

A woman is a grown-up female. When a girl grows up she becomes a woman.

My mom is a woman.

wood (noun)

Wood is the hard material in the trunk and branches of a tree. We use wood to make floors, doors, and tables.

Our kitchen floor is made of wood.

wool (noun)

Wool is a soft thread that comes from the hair of sheep and goats. We use wool to make clothes such as sweaters and gloves.

My grandma is knitting a scarf out of red wool.

worm (noun)

A worm is a small animal with a long, thin body and no legs. Worms live in the soil.

A worm wiggles through the soil.

word (noun)

A word is a group of letters or sounds with a meaning. You put together letters or sounds to make a word. You can read or write words.

Ogd is not a word but dog is.

write (verb)

You put letters or words onto paper when you write. You can write with a pencil or a pen.

Maria likes to write in her diary every day.

work (verb)

To work is to be busy doing something useful. You use energy when you work.

The farmer works hard on his farm.

wrong (adjective)

Wrong is not right. A wrong answer is not the correct one.

In the sum 12-5 = 8, the answer is wrong.

a b c d e f g h i j k l m n o p q r s t u v w x y z

x-ray (noun)
An x-ray is a special photograph. It lets a doctor see inside your body. You have to go to a hospital for an x-ray.

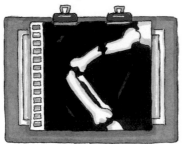

An x-ray shows if a bone is broken.

yawn (verb)
You open your mouth wide when you yawn. This lets in lots of air. People yawn when they are tired.

You yawn when you are ready to go to bed.

xylophone (noun)
A xylophone is a musical instrument. It has rows of bars that you hit with two small hammers.

Can you play a song on a xylophone?

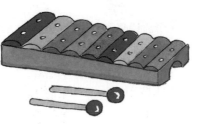

year (noun)
A year is the time it takes for the Earth to move around the Sun. There are 12 months, or 365 $\frac{1}{4}$ days, in a year.

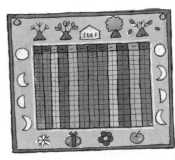

A calendar shows you how many days are in a year.

yell (verb)
To yell is to shout out loudly.

I yell when I watch a soccer game.

yelp (verb)
To yelp is to make a short, crying sound. An animal may yelp if it is hurt.

The dog yelped because its foot was hurting.

yogurt (noun)
Yogurt is a creamy food that is made from milk. Sugar and fruit can be added to yogurt.

Cherry yogurt is pink and tastes sweet.

yolk (noun)
The yolk is the yellow part in the middle of an egg.

Which part of an egg do you like best—the yolk or the white part?

young (adjective)
You are young if you were born a short time ago. Young means not old.

A baby is a young person.

yo-yo (noun)
A yo-yo is a round toy on a long piece of string. You hold the string and make the yo-yo move up and down.

You need to practice to be good with a yo-yo.

a b c d e f g h i j k l m n o p q r s t u v w x y z

Zz

zebra (noun)

A zebra is a wild animal. It looks like a horse with black and white stripes. Zebras live in Africa.

A zebra likes to eat grass.

zipper (noun)

A zipper joins two pieces of cloth together. Some clothes have a zipper instead of buttons.

I like the zipper on my coat because it is easy to zip up.

zig-zag (noun)

A zig-zag is a line with lots of points.

You make a zig-zag by going up and down with your pencil.

zoo (noun)

A zoo is a place where wild animals are kept. People go to a zoo to see the animals or to study them.

We watched the seals and the penguins at the zoo.

The alphabet

 a is for apple

b is for banana

 c is for cake

d is for dog

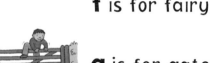 **e** is for elephant

f is for fairy

 g is for gate

h is for hat

 i is for ice cream

j is for jar

 **k** is for kite

l is for lemon

 m is for moon

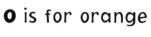 **n** is for nest

o is for orange

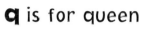 **p** is for pizza

q is for queen

 **r** is for rabbit

s is for sandcastle

 t is for teddy bear

u is for umbrella

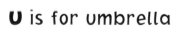 **v** is for vegetable

w is for witch

 **x** is for xylophone

y is for yo-yo

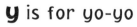 **z** is for zebra

Numbers

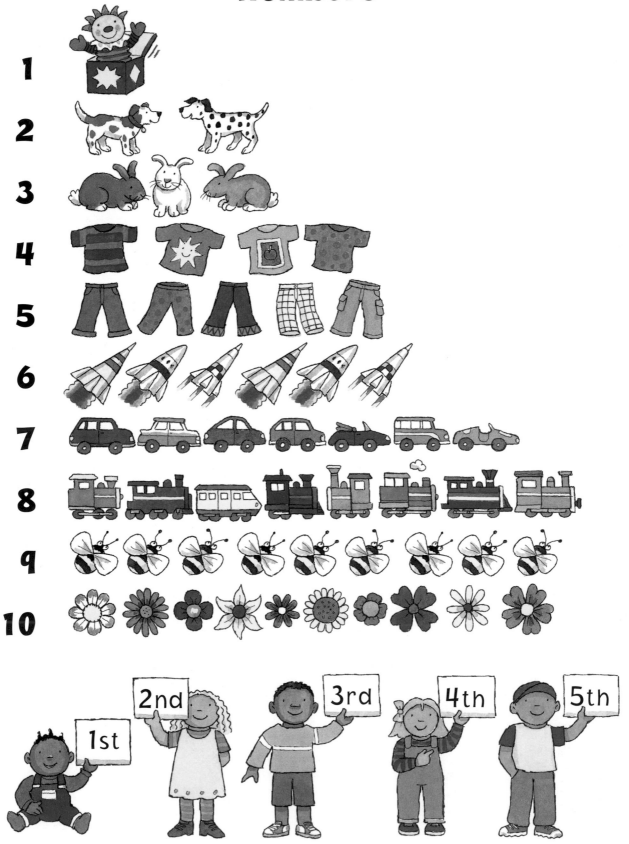

1
2
3
4
5
6
7
8
9
10

1st 2nd 3rd 4th 5th

Colors

 **green** frog

 **pink** pig

 **red** parrot

 **gray** elephant

 **orange** orang-utan

 **brown** monkey

 **white** sheep

 **black** cat

 **blue** butterfly

 **yellow** chick

 **purple** fish

216

Shapes

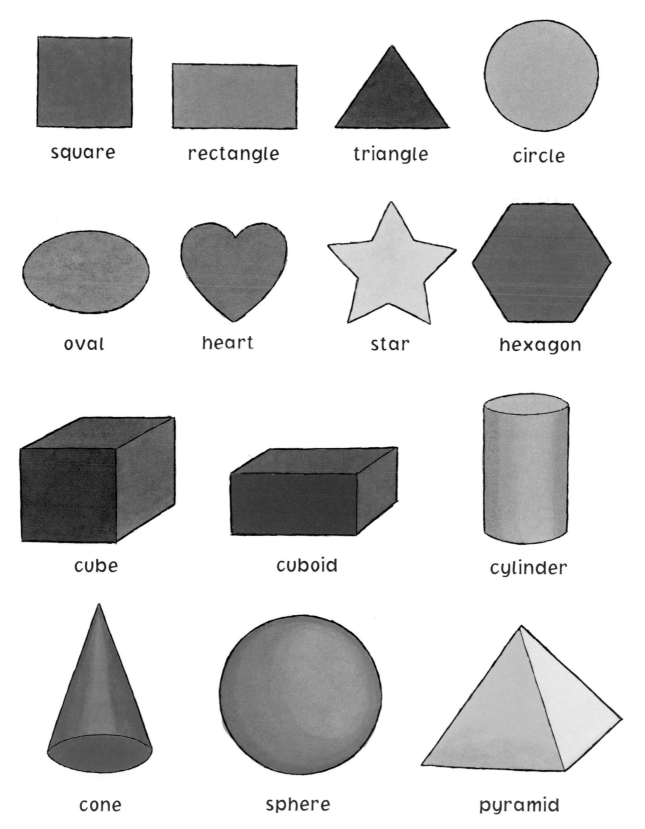

square

rectangle

triangle

circle

oval

heart

star

hexagon

cube

cuboid

cylinder

cone

sphere

pyramid

Opposites

awake

asleep

wet

dry

big

little

empty

full

fat

thin

old

new

open

shut

on

off

out

in

up

down

over

under

above

below

behind

in front of

Time

Telling the time

  seven o'clock

7:00

  quarter-past seven

7:15

  half-past seven

7:30

  quarter to eight

7:45

  twenty past nine

9:20

  ten to five

4:50

Days of the week

Sunday

Monday

Tuesday

Wednesday

Thursday

Friday

Saturday

Months of the year

January
February
March
April
May
June
July
August
September
October
November
December

Seasons

spring   summer   fall   winter